A DIVINE REVELATION OF HEALING

A DIVINE REVELATION OF HEALING

YOU, TOO, CAN RECEIVE YOUR HEALING!

Mary K. Baxter
WITH George Bloomer

WHITAKER
HOUSE

A DIVINE REVELATION OF HEALING

Mary K. Baxter
Divine Revelation, Inc.
P.O. Box 121524
Melbourne, FL 32912-1524
www.marykbaxterinc.com
E-mail: marykbaxter@yahoo.com

ISBN: 978-1-60374-117-0
Printed in the U. S. A.
© 2009 by Mary K. Baxter and
George G. Bloomer

George G. Bloomer
Bethel Family Worship Center
515 Dowd St.
Durham, NC 27701
www.bethelfamily.org

Whitaker House
1030 Hunt Valley Circle
New Kensington, PA 15068
www.whitakerhouse.com

Library of Congress Cataloging-in-Publication Data

Baxter, Mary K.
  A divine revelation of healing / Mary K. Baxter, with George G. Bloomer.
    p. cm.
  Summary: "Discusses how God desires wholeness for each of us, teaches how to receive healing from Him, and describes revelations and healings experienced or witnessed by the authors"—Provided by publisher.
  ISBN 978-1-60374-117-0 (trade pbk. : alk. paper) 1. Healing—Religious aspects—Christianity. 2. Spiritual healing. 3. Miracles. I. Bloomer, George G., 1963– II. Title.
  BT732.B34 2009
  234'.131—dc22
                            2009026957

CONTENTS

INTRODUCTION

God often works in my life through visions and revelations, and that is certainly the case when it comes to healing for His people. In many services, while I am preaching, the Lord will show me a vision of someone whom He is about to heal and the nature of that person's illness. I immediately go into private intercession because I know what the Lord is about to do.

In *A Divine Revelation of Healing*, I share true-life accounts of those who have been healed through divine intervention to lift your spirits and encourage you as you seek healing for your own personal ailments. Many times, we suffer in silence. Instead of seeking healing, we convince ourselves that our illnesses are the will of God for our lives. Yet it is the will of God for you to *"prosper in all things and be in health, just as your soul prospers"* (3 John 1:2).

Miraculous healings are recorded throughout the Bible, but many people rarely think of the possibility of healing being applicable to their ailments today. Often, when we talk about miracles, we speak of them in the past tense, as if to say that God no longer performs them. This is a falsehood that has been bred in us because, today, the church as a whole does not emphasize miracles as much as it once did.

Yet the God who did great works in former days is the same God who is ready, willing, and able to heal us today. Healing was part of God's plan in the sacrifice of His Son Jesus Christ, the benefits of which apply to all of us who believe in and receive Him. "[Jesus] *Himself bore our sins in His own body on the tree, that we, having died to sins, might live for righteousness; by whose stripes you were healed*" (1 Peter 2:24). Whatever you are going through can be turned into an opportunity for God to receive the glory. When it seems that no one is around to understand how you truly feel or even to intercede on your behalf, look to the divine Healer to be made whole.

Healing is a magnificent gift from God—one that He desires to give us, and one that He desires us to minister to others. He has entrusted this gift to us. Once we come to realize its significance and the authority we have in Christ to administer its effects, the more we will begin to enjoy spiritual, mental, emotional, and physical healing and minister the same wholeness to others.

Healing is part of God's will, desire, and promise for our lives. Regardless of the myths that you may have heard concerning healing, never doubt the fact that God wants you to be in good health. Let *A Divine Revelation of Healing* lead you to seek not only understanding of your particular condition but also the Source of your healing.

—Mary K. Baxter

A Prayer for Healing

Dear God,

We agree with the people who are holding this book today and seeking to be well, asking that they may receive complete healing as they read the pages that follow. We come against the evil principalities and powers that want to keep them from fulfilling their destinies through You, dear God, and we ask for wholeness on their behalf—spiritual, mental, emotional, and physical. May their faith increase, and may their actions reflect their new-found knowledge and experience of You as Healer. We take authority over every distraction that will attempt to hinder them from receiving their healing, and we pray that You will send Your angels as a protection over their lives. Cover them, God, as they receive their miracles from You. Let them know and believe that You are indeed a present-day Healer, and may they experience Your anointing as they seek Your face. May they not read these words simply as entertainment, but may your Word penetrate their hearts. Lord God, give them the healing they seek, and may their lives never be the same again. Let all who look upon the readers of this book be amazed by the peace of God they exhibit and by the miracle-working power taking place in their lives. In Jesus' name, amen.

—Mary K. Baxter and George G. Bloomer

Chapter 1

God's Revelation
of Himself as Healer

"I am the LORD that healeth thee."
—Exodus 15:26 (KJV)

A wonderful aspect of God's divine revelation to us as human beings—through the Scriptures and through our personal encounters with Him—is that He is our Healer.

Knowing Him as Healer

In the course of my life, God has manifested Himself to me as Healer many times. One of the first times I experienced the miracle-working power of God was when my daughter was stillborn after having been delivered by Cesarean section. There was a young intern in the room at the time, and he immediately picked her up and began administering mouth-to-mouth resuscitation. Total peace consumed the entire room as that intern worked with my baby until she finally began breathing. He handed her to the doctors and then left the room. The doctors put my daughter in an incubator, and that intern was never seen again. We felt that he was an angel of the Lord because nobody knew him, nobody could find him on staff, and he never showed up after that.

The doctors told me that if my daughter lived three days, it would be a miracle. At that time, I still hadn't received Jesus as my Savior and Lord. I had said the "sinner's prayer" many times, expressing sorrow for my sins, but I had never really received the Lord's salvation through faith. I was in my hospital room recovering from the delivery and waiting to see what would happen with my daughter when I heard a group of angels singing and calling me by my middle name. "Katherine, take Jesus as your Savior," they kept repeating. I wanted to find out where the music was coming from, but I couldn't discover its source. So, I walked over to the window, and, feeling the presence of those angels, I was led once more into the sinner's prayer and fully received the Lord right then and there. I was so excited that I pulled out the IV needles from my arms and ran down the corridor telling everybody I had been born again by the Spirit of God. The doctors assumed I was hallucinating and gave me something to put me to sleep, but I knew that God had touched me that day. He also healed my daughter. She lived, and she experienced no brain damage whatsoever.

Our God Can Do Anything!

Since then, I have seen all types of miracles and healings—from the healing of those suffering from illnesses to the deliverance of those suffering from the abuse they've inflicted upon themselves. God our Healer desires to make us whole in body, mind, and spirit, and He has called me to minister healing and wholeness to others as I preach His gospel of salvation. At times, I minister to drug addicts, and I have seen hundreds delivered from their addictions, because it is God doing the healing, not me. I have laid my hands on those addicted to crack cocaine and watched as God miraculously set them free.

God our Healer desires to make us whole in body, mind, and spirit.

In many of the miracles I've encountered, God's angels showed me how to pray. This type of revelation is part of my ministry, which includes dreams and visions. I'll actually see angels next to people, and they will show me where the person needs prayer. For example, I'll be able to see inside a person's chest, and the angel will put his hand on the chest and show me a dark spot on his or her lungs. Then, I'll see God's Word written out—words such as "By My stripes, you are healed" (see 1 Peter 2:24) and "*I am the* LORD *that healeth thee*" (Exodus 15:26 KJV). After that, I'll see the Word turn into a sword that goes to the place where the person needs healing, and I'll see the fire and the healing power of God go into it.

God has given me dreams, visions, and revelations in order to help people. They aren't just for the sake of my family and me. They're for everybody. Our God can do anything! We just have to recognize how great and compassionate He is.

We serve a God who can replace whatever is missing in your life. In whatever area you need healing, God is waiting and willing to heal you and to meet your need. I know what I am talking about because I have experienced it firsthand. For example, my son had epilepsy, causing some of his brain cells to be destroyed. After he was diagnosed with epilepsy, we had to go for follow-up appointments with doctors every six months. We were praying for healing, and, over time, God miraculously restored those brain cells! Several doctors confirmed that the cells were now normal. They were amazed at this miracle and admitted, "It took the power of God for this to happen."

God said, "*I will restore to you the years that the swarming locust has eaten, the crawling locust, the consuming locust, and the chewing locust, My great army which I sent among you*" (Joel 2:25). If you need Him to restore something in your life, do not be afraid to ask Him. God can restore everything that our enemy, the devil, has taken from our lives. Jesus said, "*The thief does not come except to steal, and to kill, and to destroy. I have come that they may have life, and that they may have it more abundantly*" (John 10:10).

Healing for Spirit, Soul, and Body

The word *heal*, according to *Merriam Webster's 11th Collegiate Dictionary*, means:

+ To make sound or whole.

+ To cause (an undesirable condition) to be overcome.

+ To restore to original purity or integrity.

These definitions draw attention to the fact that sickness—and God's healing—is not limited to physical issues. It applies to our entire beings—spiritual, mental, emotional, and physical. God desires us to be whole in every aspect of our lives. "*Now may the God of peace Himself sanctify you completely; and may your whole **spirit**, **soul**, and **body** be preserved blameless at the coming of our Lord Jesus Christ. He who calls you is faithful, who also will do it*" (1 Thessalonians 5:23–24, emphasis added).

In the book of John, Jesus encountered a man who was an invalid, and He asked him, *"Wilt thou be made whole?"* (John 5:6 KJV). This man had been ill for thirty-eight years and had undoubtedly become very frustrated mentally and emotionally over the toll that his physical illness was taking upon his body. Jesus was asking the man if he wanted Him to overcome the condition and make him whole.

It has been my experience that when people are prayed for, they sometimes receive more than one type of healing at the same time. For instance, a man named Adrian attended one of my meetings and received both emotional and physical healing. He had sat at the rear of the church because his back was in such pain due to an injury he'd sustained in a car accident several months earlier. He wrote to me, "After you prayed the prayer of faith, the spirit of healing was released in the room. I was healed from unforgiveness, bitterness from the past, sinus problems, back pain, and, to top it off, about five teeth were refilled in my mouth. I cried like a baby that night but left the church service with peace, joy, deliverance, and healing."

When people are prayed for, they sometimes receive more than one type of healing at the same time.

The Scriptures Reveal God as Healer

It is not only by the personal experiences of others and ourselves that we understand God's healing power. By the truth of God's Word, we can know for certain that He is our Healer. He revealed this attribute in the Scriptures through the life of Abraham and continued to reveal it through His covenant with the people of Israel.

This revelation culminated in the sacrifice of His Son Jesus Christ on our behalf. Since the fall of humanity, God has been unfolding His plan of salvation and restoration in Christ for rebellious and broken human beings. This plan includes not only deliverance from sin and eternal death, but also healing for our bodies and minds.

Old Testament Revelation and Manifestations

Among the first healings mentioned in the Bible were those in which God restored women's ability to conceive children. (See Genesis 20:17–18.) The patriarch Abraham's wife, Sarah, also received a healing and miracle regarding childbearing. After years of being barren, and when she was past normal childbearing age, she was enabled to conceive the promised child, Isaac, at the age of ninety, as part of God's covenant promise to Abraham that He would make him a great nation. (See Genesis 17:15–19; 21:1–3.)

God revealed to the Israelites His nature as Healer and promised them divine health if they kept His commandments. When He brought the nation of Israel out of slavery in Egypt, after inflicting their captors with ten plagues, He told the people,

> *If you diligently heed the voice of the LORD your God and do what is right in His sight, give ear to His commandments and keep all His statutes, I will put none of the diseases on you which I have brought on the Egyptians. For I am the LORD who heals you.*
>
> (Exodus 15:26)

> *Then it shall come to pass, because you listen to these judgments, and keep and do them, that the LORD your*

God will keep with you the covenant and the mercy which He swore to your fathers. And He will love you and bless you and multiply you; He will also bless the fruit of your womb and the fruit of your land, your grain and your new wine and your oil, the increase of your cattle and the offspring of your flock, in the land of which He swore to your fathers to give you. You shall be blessed above all peoples; there shall not be a male or female barren among you or among your livestock. And the LORD will take away from you all sickness, and will afflict you with none of the terrible diseases of Egypt which you have known.

(Deuteronomy 7:12–15)

King David wrote about God's healing power:

Bless the LORD, O my soul, and forget not all His benefits: who forgives all your iniquities, who heals all your diseases, who redeems your life from destruction, who crowns you with lovingkindness and tender mercies. (Psalm 103:2–4)

O LORD, do not rebuke me in Your anger, nor chasten me in Your hot displeasure. Have mercy on me, O LORD, for I am weak; O LORD, heal me, for my bones are troubled. (Psalm 6:1–2)

Blessed is he who considers the poor; the LORD will deliver him in time of trouble. The LORD will preserve him and keep him alive, and he will be blessed on the earth; You will not deliver him to the will of his enemies. The LORD will strengthen him on his bed of illness; You will sustain him on his sickbed. I said,

"LORD, *be merciful to me; heal my soul, for I have sinned against You.*" (Psalm 41:1–4)

God showed His mercy not only to His people, the Israelites, but also to others who came to Him seeking healing. In 1 and 2 Kings, we read how God raised two boys from the dead by the prophets Elijah and Elisha. (See 1 Kings 17:8–24; 2 Kings 4:8–37.) In 2 Kings, we read the account of Naaman, the commander of the army of the king of Syria, whom God healed of leprosy through the prophet Elisha. (See 2 Kings 5:1–15.)

The book of Daniel records the divine health that God gave to Daniel and his three companions because they honored Him, even though they were captives in Babylon and had faced pressure to compromise their faith. (See Daniel 1:1–15.)

There are many more examples in the Old Testament of God's healing power. Yet the full revelation and provision of God as Healer came in the person of His Son Jesus Christ.

New Testament Revelation and Manifestations

Jesus was God the Healer coming to earth to restore humanity's relationship with Himself and to restore humanity to wholeness in His image. When He was on earth, Jesus fulfilled this prophesy through His life:

The Spirit of the LORD is upon Me, because He has anointed Me to preach the gospel to the poor; He has sent Me to heal the brokenhearted, to proclaim liberty to the captives and recovery of sight to the blind, to set at liberty those who are oppressed. (Luke 4:18)

Again, the gospel of salvation is one of healing for the whole person: spirit, soul, and body.

The next day John saw Jesus coming toward him, and said, "Behold! The Lamb of God who takes away the sin of the world!" (John 1:29)

When evening had come, they brought to Him many who were demon-possessed. And He cast out the spirits with a word, and healed all who were sick, that it might be fulfilled which was spoken by Isaiah the prophet, saying: "He Himself took our infirmities and bore our sicknesses." (Matthew 8:16–17)

The Purpose of Jesus' Sacrifice

Just as salvation from sin comes through Christ, healing comes through Him, as well. To understand and receive healing, we must remain focused on the purpose of Jesus' sacrifice for us. He did not bear our sorrows and sins for nothing. Let us look at the significance of Jesus' suffering on our behalf through a description of His sacrifice in Isaiah 53:4–5:

Surely He has borne our griefs and carried our sorrows; yet we esteemed Him stricken, smitten by God, and afflicted. But He was wounded for our transgressions, He was bruised for our iniquities; the chastisement for our peace was upon Him, and by His stripes we are healed.

1. *"He was wounded for our transgressions"*: The torment that Jesus bore on the cross was not for Himself but for us, because He was without sin. *"For we do not have a High*

Priest who cannot sympathize with our weaknesses, but was in all points tempted as we are, yet without sin" (Hebrews 4:15). What if we had to pay the price for every transgression we ever committed? *"Whoever shall keep the whole law, and yet stumble in one point, he is guilty of all"* (James 2:10). Jesus bore the penalty for us so that we would not have to pay it. *"The wages of sin is death, but the gift of God is eternal life in Christ Jesus our Lord"* (Romans 6:23).

2. *"He was bruised for our iniquities"*: What if every time we sinned, we were beaten with a lash across our backs? Before long, we might faint at the mere thought of it. Thankfully, the price for our sins has already been paid. Jesus took the pain and punishment of our sins upon Himself. *"Looking unto Jesus, the author and finisher of our faith, who for the joy that was set before Him endured the cross, despising the shame, and has sat down at the right hand of the throne of God"* (Hebrews 12:2).

3. *"The chastisement for our peace was upon Him"*: Not only did Jesus take the punishment for our sins, securing our peace with God the Father, but He also took on the responsibility of guarding our peace.

> It [righteousness] *shall be imputed to us who believe in Him* [God] *who raised up Jesus our Lord from the dead, who was delivered up because of our offenses, and was raised because of our justification. Therefore, having been justified by faith, we have peace with God through our Lord Jesus Christ, through whom also we have access by faith into this grace in which we stand.*
> (Romans 4:24–5:2)

> *Be anxious for nothing, but in everything by prayer and supplication, with thanksgiving, let your requests*

be made known to God; and the peace of God, which surpasses all understanding, will guard your hearts and minds through Christ Jesus.   (Philippians 4:6–7)

Today, Jesus continues to defeat the attacks of the enemy on our behalf, reminding us that He has already won the war and that peace is our inheritance. Furthermore, when we become so bogged down in our difficulties that we forget we have the victory, God's Holy Spirit *"also helps in our weaknesses. For we do not know what we should pray for as we ought, but the Spirit Himself makes intercession for us with groanings which cannot be uttered"* (Romans 8:26).

Jesus continues to defeat the attacks of the enemy on our behalf.

4. *"By His stripes we are healed"*: The result of such a great and miraculous sacrifice is that by His stripes, His wounds, His bruises, we are healed!

Eternal Healing

We may sometimes experience the need for physical, emotional, and mental healing while we live on this earth. Yet, because of Jesus' sacrifice for us, there will come a day when we will be absolutely whole and never have to worry about sorrow or sickness again. One of Jesus' disciples, John, wrote in the book of Revelation,

Then I, John, saw the holy city, New Jerusalem, coming down out of heaven from God, prepared as a bride adorned for her husband. And I heard a loud voice from heaven saying, "Behold, the tabernacle of God is with men, and He will dwell with them, and they shall

be His people. God Himself will be with them and be their God. And God will wipe away every tear from their eyes; there shall be no more death, nor sorrow, nor crying. There shall be no more pain, for the former things have passed away." Then He who sat on the throne said, "Behold, I make all things new." And He said to me, "Write, for these words are true and faithful." And He said to me, "It is done! I am the Alpha and the Omega, the Beginning and the End. I will give of the fountain of the water of life freely to him who thirsts. He who overcomes shall inherit all things, and I will be his God and he shall be My son."

(Revelation 21:2–7)

What a blessed promise this is to us! No more pain, sorrow, crying, or death. We will be perfectly healed and ready to spend eternity with God.

Yet even now, on earth, we can receive healing through the power of God at work in our lives. It is my desire through this book that you will not only come to understand that God is Healer, but also have a personal revelation that He is *your* Healer.

Chapter 2

BROKEN AND WOUNDED HUMANITY

*"[Jesus] Himself bore our sins in His own body on the tree,
that we, having died to sins, might live for righteousness; by
whose stripes you were healed"*
—1 Peter 2:24

Sickness and disease seem to plague our nation and our world. Adults are dealing with sicknesses such as Alzheimer's, chronic arthritis, heart disease, breast cancer, HPV, diabetes, and cancer, as well as with psychological problems like chronic depression, schizophrenia, bipolar disorder, and obsessive-compulsive disorder, all of which attack people's mental stability. People are broken physically, mentally, and emotionally.

Sadly, children are being *born* with illnesses and other physical problems, such as asthma, congestive heart failure, lung and kidney infections, blindness, and deafness. They are sometimes even born with such diseases as tuberculosis or AIDS. They may suffer withdrawal from addictions they inherited from their parents' own addictions to crack, methamphetamine, and other destructive substances.

One result is that pharmaceutical companies are developing pills and other medicines to address almost every physical and emotional ailment imaginable—a pill to wake up, to go to sleep, to laugh, to keep from crying, to treat headaches, colds, backaches, and coughs. They've created creams and medicated lotions to alleviate the discomfort of eczema and other skin conditions.

The pharmaceutical industry is a one-hundred-billion-dollar business, yet it seems as if many people aren't getting well or are getting sicker. As people's bodies become immune to treatments, stronger medicinal solutions are developed to take their places. Some diseases persist because they are mainly the result of people's unhealthy lifestyles. And while health care is big business, many people can't afford it. Except for the grace of God, some of these people would no longer be alive.

What Is Your Diagnosis?

Sickness is not just about societal conditions and statistics. It can be very personal. What is your ailment? Do you or does someone close to you need a healing?

When someone visits a physician regarding an ailment, the first thing the doctor does is to ask a series of questions. He or she is gathering as much information as possible in order to reveal the nature of the illness that is causing the discomfort. This is because the doctor knows that just treating the surface symptoms is not enough. If there is a medical cure for your ailment, the doctor's job is to identify the antidote to bring about that cure through prescriptions, treatments, surgery, and so forth.

Whether it is physical, mental, emotional, or spiritual healing that you are in need of, you must be honest regarding your symptoms. So let's begin to make a diagnosis by simply asking a series of questions.

1. Are you physically ill, and if so, what are your symptoms? God works healing through doctors, as well as directly, so have you shared all of your symptoms openly and honestly with a reputable physician? Furthermore, have you been as open and transparent as possible when asked about certain behaviors? One of the things that many physicians stress is the need for honest communication between patient and doctor in order to procure the best treatment possible. For instance, many people, when asked, "Describe your daily diet," often respond with very vague and nondescript answers: "Oh, a light breakfast…light lunch…small dinner at night…not much snacking between meals." If you eat bacon and sausage each morning with a side of eggs and toast and wash it all down with a mocha latte, admit it. Don't allow embarrassment to keep you from the healing that you so desperately need. Doctors are accustomed to hearing the worst, so if you go to them for treatment, prepare to divulge the truth. Don't allow pride to cause you to fall further into an abyss from which only aggressive medical treatment may pull you out in the future. *"Pride goes before destruction"* (Proverbs 16:18). You cannot adequately present the message of Christ to others when you are purposefully doing things to your own body to hinder you from being effective for God. *"Do you not know that your body is the temple of the Holy Spirit who is in you, whom you have from God, and you are not your own? For you were bought at a price; therefore glorify God in your body and in your spirit, which are God's"* (1 Corinthians 6:19–20).

2. Are your symptoms mental or emotional? Are you withdrawn from friends and loved ones, and if so, why? What events led up to this behavior? Is this something new that you are experiencing, or have you always felt this way—

We need to surround ourselves with those who believe in our God and can remind us of His power.

what many refer to as "depressed" or "down in the dumps"? Sometimes, events occur in our lives that send our emotions and sense of security spiraling out of control, and if we don't talk to someone about how we feel, they may get worse. Especially as children of God, we need to surround ourselves with those of like faith, those who believe in our God and can remind us of His power whenever we become weak.

"And let us consider one another in order to stir up love and good works, not forsaking the assembling of ourselves together, as is the manner of some, but exhorting one another, and so much the more as you see the Day approaching" (Hebrews 10:24–25).

Some people simply do not know why they feel the way that they do, and this sometimes has to do with a chemical imbalance in their bodies or other physical complications for which a licensed doctor can prescribe a treatment. For others, it could be a strategic demonic attack brought about to hinder their progress as they go about doing the Father's business. We must remain on guard spiritually at all times, because the devil continually seeks our moments of vulnerability to wreak havoc in our lives: *"Be sober, be vigilant; because your adversary the devil walks about like a roaring lion, seeking whom he may devour. Resist him, steadfast in the faith"* (1 Peter 5:8–9).

3. Are your symptoms spiritual? Do you have a relationship with God? Do you know that your sins have been forgiven and that you are His child?

If you have had a relationship with God, does it now feel as if He has forgotten about you? Does it seem as if your prayers hit the ceiling and bounce off? At one time or another in our spiritual walks with God, we all will feel as if our prayers aren't being answered or that God does not care. As our faith is being tried and tested, God wants us to stand these tests and not fall beneath the pressures of them.

A mother who is teaching her child to walk will sometimes allow the child to fall so that the young one is no longer fearful of stepping out and attempting to walk on his or her own. Each time the child falls, he or she looks to Mom because the child has built a relationship with the mother that has led to the knowledge, "I might fall, but I know my mother is not going to allow me to cause harm to myself in the process. I trust her." A similar scenario is true in our relationships with the heavenly Father. God allows us to go through certain experiences in life so that we will learn to step out in faith and trust Him. If we were constantly afraid of hurting ourselves, we would never step out in faith and grow or reach new levels in life. Therefore, God allows us to go through a number of experiences to teach us to stand against the tactics of the devil. *"Finally, my brethren, be strong in the Lord and in the power of His might. Put on the whole armor of God, that you may be able to stand against the wiles of the devil"* (Ephesians 6:10–11).

We are in the fight of our lives, but this battle is not in the natural; it is spiritual. If you could see in the spirit realm, you would know how Satan and his cohorts strategize to try to remain one step ahead of us. The devil wants to divert our attention away from God, and he will use any means to do so.

By His Stripes, We Are Healed

God does not want us walking around carrying illnesses and diseases that we do not have to bear. If He did, then He would not have sent His only Son Jesus to die for us, for it is by the stripes that He endured on the cross that we were healed. Adam and Eve, the first human beings, were created whole—without sickness, disease, or mental and emotional distress. God's provision of healing is a result of His love and salvation through Christ. "[Jesus] *Himself bore our sins in His own body on the tree, that we, having died to sins, might live for righteousness; by whose stripes you were healed*" (1 Peter 2:24). This means that for whatever ailments we face, and for whatever sicknesses that our enemy, the devil, tries to afflict us with, God has already prepared a cure. Hallelujah!

The body of Christ must learn that believers hold "*the authority to trample on serpents and scorpions, and over all the power of the enemy*" (Luke 10:19), and that, in Jesus' name, "*they will lay hands on the sick, and they will recover*" (Mark 16:18). It's no small wonder that Christians are often able to sustain unimaginable strength in the midst of some of the most grueling circumstances. Jesus promised that "*nothing shall by any means hurt* [us]" (Luke 10:19). This does not mean that we will not experience adversities in life, but that with each struggle, God will bear us up on eagles' wings and allow us to endure the turbulence as we journey toward the other side of the storm. (See Exodus 19:4.)

The Bible is full of accounts of miraculous healing, but unfortunately, many people think that healing is an impossibility for the time and day in which we live. That is a deception of the devil. He wants us to believe that the era of supernatural healing is a lost phenomenon. If we are not careful, we will buy into his lies. Many people have lost their faith and given in to the notion that the records of miraculous healings we read about in the Bible are simply fairy tales and are neither literal nor applicable to real life. What would happen, however, if we all took the time to actually embrace the fact that these biblical accounts were true-life encounters and that God is still performing the same types of miracles today? The power of God would be released, and we would begin experiencing the manifestation of the supernatural as never before. Incurable diseases would be healed, mysterious ailments would cease, blind eyes would see, and deaf ears would open. My prayer is that the church of Jesus Christ will experience a yearning for the full manifestation of supernatural healings.

God is still performing the same types of miracles that we read about in the Bible.

Hold On to the Word of God

One of the most common hindrances preventing many of us from experiencing this supernatural outpouring is lack of faith. God can do anything that is in His will to perform and that aligns with His Word. So why not trust Him to do something that we are unable to do for ourselves? I am not suggesting that we clean out our medicine cabinets, reject the doctor's orders, and ignore professional medical advice, but that we should employ faith and apply the Word of God to our lives as we are also utilizing medical intervention and treatments.

Hearing a bad diagnosis about one's health is often a faith killer, but my prayer is that after you read this book, you will refuse to accept bad news as a death sentence. Whether you are believing God for a miracle for yourself or for your loved ones, hold on to the Word of God, regardless of how things seem in the natural. If you hear bad news, receive it as an opportunity to see the full manifestation of the Spirit of God—who is active today—working in your life or in the lives of your loved ones.

Many Christians have heard the saying "Hold on to God" so often that they now receive these words merely as a cliché instead of viable words of encouragement. However, if we would just allow God's words about healing to penetrate our spirits, and actually do what the Word of God says instead of just hearing it (see James 1:22), we would begin to witness seemingly impossible healings manifested right before our eyes.

Ready to Minister Healing to Others

As a minister of the gospel, I am constantly approached by those requesting prayer for healing. Regardless of the particular need, my desire is to introduce each person to the power of God—the true Source of life and everything else. This is also my purpose in writing *A Divine Revelation of Healing*. I would like to introduce you to the Source of your healing and also to His power to heal. Even those who already know God the Father are not always acquainted with His desire and ability to heal them through His Son Jesus Christ. I strongly encourage you to explore God's Word to discover His commitment to us of complete healing—inward and outward—and to receive His healing. Once we receive the gift of healing for ourselves, we are more likely to pass along the promise of this gift to others.

I believe we are rapidly approaching the last days before Christ returns to the earth and that many people will come to the church seeking from God what they are unable to find from humankind's intervention. This includes healing. Whether their needs are spiritual, mental, emotional, or physical, we must be prepared to supply the biblical answers that lead to the healing of the wounds of those who seek complete freedom from their ailments. The question is, Will the church be prepared to lead the influx of seekers to the One whom they ultimately seek? *"When the Son of Man comes, will He really find faith on the earth?"* (Luke 18:8).

We must never seek personal glory for God's miraculous works. (See Isaiah 42:8.) Instead, in all things, we must lead those who seek healing to the One who can heal all their wounds. If someone who was ill came to you today, would you, as a Christian, be prepared to pray for this person and see him or her recover (see Mark 16:18), or would you be at a loss for words…unprepared to minister the healing of Christ?

The "laying on of hands" for healing is essentially a spiritual connection between the person needing God's healing power, ourselves, and God. When a believer is walking according

When a believer is walking according to the Spirit of God, he or she is a mediator through which God's healing power comes.

to the Spirit of God, he or she is a mediator or channel through which God's healing power comes to an individual who is ailing from sickness or disease. Can you imagine going to someone on his sickbed, laying your hands on him, and watching as he gets up out of the bed completely healed? If this scenario seems utterly unimaginable to you, then read on. Not only does God still heal as He did in former days, but we can walk in the power of healing as Jesus did when He was on earth, also. Jesus told us, "*Most assuredly, I say to you, he who believes in Me, the works that I do he will do also; and greater works than these he will do, because I go to My Father*" (John 14:12).

Chapter 3

HEALING FOR THE SPIRIT

*"But to you who fear My name the Sun of Righteousness shall
arise with healing in His wings."*
—Malachi 4:2

God created each of us with a spirit, a soul (including the mind, will, and emotions), and a body. (See
1 Thessalonians 5:23.) While each of these areas of our
lives is important, spiritual healing is of primary importance and leads to ultimate healing in the other areas.

After God created the first human beings, they rebelled
against Him and allowed sin to rule their lives and to enter
the world. Since that time, humanity has been a race that
is dead, spiritually speaking: *"Through one man sin entered
the world, and death through sin, and thus death spread to all
men, because all sinned"* (Romans 5:12). Unless a human
being applies God's remedy for sin and death, he or she remains in this spiritually dead state. But God has provided
spiritual healing for us through faith in Jesus! *"Therefore we
were buried with Him through baptism into death, that just as*

Christ was raised from the dead by the glory of the Father, even so we also should walk in newness of life" (Romans 6:4).

What does it mean to receive spiritual healing? First, spiritual healing involves renewing your spirit—your essential self as a human being made in God's image—from the corruption of sin so that you can experience spiritual wholeness and eternal life. *"But now having been set free from sin, and having become slaves of God, you have your fruit to holiness, and the end, everlasting life. For the wages of sin is death, but the gift of God is eternal life in Christ Jesus our Lord"* (Romans 6:22–23). Eternal life includes forgiveness for all our sins. *"To open their eyes, in order to turn them from darkness to light, and from the power of Satan to God, that they may receive forgiveness of sins and an inheritance among those who are sanctified by faith in Me [Jesus]"* (Acts 26:18).

Second, spiritual healing includes restoring the relationship between you and God that was broken as the result of sin and spiritual death. *"Therefore, having been justified by faith, we have peace with God through our Lord Jesus Christ"* (Romans 5:1). When that relationship is restored, you become *"born again."* (See John 3:1–21.) You become God's child. *"But as many as received Him, to them He gave the right to become children of God, to those who believe in His name: who were born, not of blood, nor of the will of the flesh, nor of the will of man, but of God"* (John 1:12–13).

To be made whole spiritually means that you can now enter into all the promises of God's Word that apply to His children.

Third, to be made whole spiritually means that you can now enter into all the promises of God's Word that apply to those who are His children. *"The Spirit Himself bears witness with our spirit that we are children of God, and if children, then heirs; heirs of God and joint heirs with Christ, if indeed we suffer with Him, that we may also be glorified together"* (Romans 8:16–17). *"For all the promises of God in Him are Yes, and in Him Amen, to the glory of God through us"* (2 Corinthians 1:20).

Salvation and Healing

Forgiveness of sins can pave the way for physical and emotional healing, especially if sin has caused an illness. In the ninth chapter of Matthew, when Jesus ministered to a paralyzed man, He dealt with both spiritual and physical healing in his life.

> *Then behold, they brought to Him* [Jesus] *a paralytic lying on a bed. When Jesus saw their faith, He said to the paralytic, "Son, be of good cheer; your sins are forgiven you." And at once some of the scribes said within themselves, "This Man blasphemes!" But Jesus, knowing their thoughts, said, "Why do you think evil in your hearts? For which is easier, to say, 'Your sins are forgiven you,' or to say, 'Arise and walk'? But that you may know that the Son of Man has power on earth to forgive sins"; then He said to the paralytic, "Arise, take up your bed, and go to your house." And he arose and departed to his house.* (Matthew 9:2–7)

The Greek word that literally means "to heal" is *sozo.* This word is also commonly translated "to save." Many times throughout the Bible, when God healed someone, He would also forgive his or her sins. This is not to imply that everyone who is sick has a specific sin to blame for his or her condition, but only to emphasize God's commitment to our complete healing—body, soul, and spirit.

How amazing it must have felt for the man sitting at the gate called Beautiful in Acts 3, who had been lame since birth, to expect to receive a few coins to live on yet to be given something much greater—health and wholeness! As he sat there begging for alms from those entering the temple, he spotted Peter and John and asked them for money. Peter and John replied, *"Silver and gold I do not have, but what I do have I give you: In the name of Jesus Christ of Nazareth, rise up and walk"* (verse 6).

There are thousands of wealthy people whose money cannot buy health and wholeness, either physical, mental, emotional, or spiritual. Often, we look at those who are rich and wonder, *How can they be so unhappy with all that money?* Money really does not buy true happiness or wholeness. These things can be acquired only through receiving spiritual healing from a restored relationship with God the Father.

In receiving spiritual healing, therefore, you can acquire the power to receive the mental, emotional, and physical healing you need, as well. Whether this healing is activated through medicinal means or supernatural means, healing in all its aspects is a gift from God. If you have ever doubted that God desires His best for you, then open your mind to a new way of thinking. Indeed, you can be made whole through the healing power of almighty God!

Be anxious for nothing, but in everything by prayer and supplication, with thanksgiving, let your requests be made known to God; and the peace of God, which

*surpasses all understanding, will guard your hearts and
minds through Christ Jesus.* (Philippians 4:6–7)

Allow God's peace, which surpasses all human understanding, to be your portion as you seek Him and receive
the healing that you need. Without spiritual peace, it is
often difficult to adequately begin the physical or emotional healing process effectively, because anxiety and lack
of faith can block it. To some, it may seem unheard of to
expect peace in the midst of suffering, but with God, all
things are possible. (See Matthew 19:26; Mark 10:27.)

The Reality of Spiritual Death

The consequences of refusing healing for the spirit
and remaining in spiritual death are unthinkable: eternal
corruption of our spirits and an eternity apart from God.
Years ago, when Jesus first appeared to me in visions and
revelations at night, He told me that He was going to take
me on a journey with Him to hell. After showing me the
compartments of hell, He would then show me heaven.

Jesus also told me that I would see horrible things in
hell that I would write in a book to help people all over the
world receive salvation and escape an eternity separated
from God. I have traveled to about ninety nations bringing
this message, and today, souls are still being saved by the
thousands after hearing my testimony or reading about it
in my books.[1]

Before taking me to hell, Jesus raised His hand, and the
roof of my home rolled back. My spirit seemed to come out
of my body, and I stood beside the Lord. Although my body

[1] See Mary K. Baxter, *A Divine Revelation of Hell* and *A Divine Revelation of Heaven*
(New Kensington, PA: Whitaker House).

lay in the bed in a sleeplike state, my spirit was awake and knew everything ten times sharper outside of my body. Jesus took hold of my hand, and we rose up into the galaxies. I saw a scroll with Psalm 91 written on it hanging over my house, and three ranks of angels surrounded my home. Some of the angels were very tall and had long swords. If anything evil came near my house, the angels would take their swords and cremate the darkness. Warfare angels are all around us, and if you call upon God, He will send you help.

Jesus and I then began to go down a "gateway" that led to hell. There was a gray wall, and behind it were demon powers by the thousands. I saw demons that looked like cockroaches about twelve feet tall, along with spiders that were just as huge. Demons with razors on their backs roamed about. The cockroaches are the perverse demons in the world. Many people do not realize we are fighting a spiritual war with unseen evil forces.

As Jesus and I went down this gateway, I could hear millions of voices screaming, "Let me die! Let me die! No man cares for my soul!" As far as I could see, there were pits of fire in the ground, and in every pit was a skeleton. These were people who had died and were reaping what that they had sown on the earth.

A watered-down gospel has been preached so much that people no longer know about the torments of hell. The book of Daniel talks about the truth being *"cast…down to the ground"* (see Daniel 8:12), and that is the hour we are in right now. The truth of God's Word is being cast to the ground, and people are replacing it with a watered-down gospel that lacks the power to work a spiritual transformation in their lives. You need to know that when it feels good to sin, the devil is trying to destroy you. Now is the time to seek God's spiritual life, health, and wholeness—because in hell, this will no longer be possible.

Now is the time to seek God's spiritual life, health, and wholeness.

In hell, I heard voices crying out to Jesus, but He told me it was too late for those souls because the judgment of His Father had already been set. I heard the voice of a man crying out, "I've been here for fifty years. I try to escape this torment, but demons grab me and stab me and pull me apart and I scream for the other part of my body." The horrors of hell— we don't even know them all! Hell reeks of vile odors, like the odors of a sewer. My heart broke as I listened helplessly to the gnashing of teeth and to the crying out of souls who regretted that they had not listened to the warnings of the sincere preachers of God.

I saw the skeletal remains of one woman, and her voice cried out, "Lord, I'll do right if You'll let me out of hell! I don't want to be here anymore. I heard Your words of repentance and love when I was on the earth. I remember my family upon the earth, and some of them have come here. I remember the gospel that was preached to me. Every day, the pits get fuller. Lord, please get me out of here!"

Jesus began to cry, and she began to cry. He said to her, "The judgment of My Father has been set. It's too late." And as Jesus and I walked on, I heard a multitude of voices of doomed souls continuing to cry out in anguish to Him as He passed by.

While we are here on the earth, we have to stop being afraid of the big "puff of wind" that the devil is blowing, because that's all he is compared with God's power—just wind. We have to turn to the ways of God right now because in hell, there is no escape. When the people in hell try to climb out of the pit, the demons shove them back down and burn them even more. These demons have absolutely no mercy. They torment the souls, saying, "We deceived you...we deceived you!" Many church leaders do not want to talk about hell because they don't want their congregations to become upset. I am sure that those who are suffering in hell would love to tell these leaders that it is worth the risk of upsetting people to keep them from a horrid eternity.

I looked at the masses of souls in the heart of hell. That was not God's desire for human beings. At first, God made hell for the devil and his angels, who had rebelled against Him. *"God did not spare the angels who sinned, but cast them down to hell and delivered them into chains of darkness, to be reserved for judgment"* (2 Peter 2:4). However, all human beings who rebel against God and refuse to repent before they die will also end up there. Jesus said, *"Do not fear those who kill the body but cannot kill the soul. But rather fear Him who is able to destroy both soul and body in hell"* (Matthew 10:28). Eternal death and punishment are the destiny of the devil, demons, and every person who has not received salvation through Jesus Christ and lived for Him.

> *Then* [Jesus] *will also say to those on the left hand, "Depart from Me, you cursed, into the everlasting fire prepared for the devil and his angels."*
>
> (Matthew 25:41)

> *The devil, who deceived them, was cast into the lake of fire and brimstone where the beast and the false prophet*

are. And they will be tormented day and night forever and ever. Then I saw a great white throne and Him who sat on it, from whose face the earth and the heaven fled away. And there was found no place for them. And I saw the dead, small and great, standing before God, and books were opened. And another book was opened, which is the Book of Life. And the dead were judged according to their works, by the things which were written in the books. The sea gave up the dead who were in it, and Death and Hades delivered up the dead who were in them. And they were judged, each one according to his works. Then Death and Hades were cast into the lake of fire. This is the second death. And anyone not found written in the Book of Life was cast into the lake of fire.   (Revelation 20:10–15)

Jesus said, *"If your right hand causes you to sin, cut it off and cast it from you; for it is more profitable for you that one of your members perish, than for your whole body to be cast into hell"* (Matthew 5:30). Of course, He didn't mean that you should physically maim yourself. He meant that it is better to get rid of what causes you to sin while you are on the earth than to risk allowing it to cause you eternal suffering. To rid yourself of what causes you to sin means to give up whatever is keeping you from God and appeasing your fleshly nature and to actively pursue what is pleasing to God. Let it go! Nothing is worth holding on to that causes you to jeopardize your spiritual standing with God. Cut it out of your life completely. You never want to allow yourself to hold on to a habit, a way of thinking, a certain behavior, a relationship, or anything that will cause you to miss out on eternal salvation.

In hell, I saw entrances between hell and earth that would open and shut. Demons would come out of them and go into the earth to torment. Everywhere we look is one opportunity after another to appease the sinful desires of the flesh rather than cling to God. The Scriptures tell us,

> *Therefore submit to God. Resist the devil and he will flee from you. Draw near to God and He will draw near to you. Cleanse your hands, you sinners; and purify your hearts, you double-minded….Humble yourselves in the sight of the Lord, and He will lift you up.*
> (James 4:7–8, 10)

The devil is very cunning in his tactics to entice us from God. That is why we must remember that not everything that sounds good on the surface is of God.

Ezekiel 28 describes a being who apparently is Satan. Before Satan fell, he walked with God, and the workmanship of his "pipes" was created in him as the anointed cherub. (See verses 13–18.) After evil was found in him and he was cast out of heaven, Satan used his abilities to uncover the sins of human beings, accuse them, and whisper his deceitful lies to them. His intention is to tempt people into killing themselves before the Spirit of God can cleanse them from their sins, save their souls, and restore their peace.

In my revelations of hell, I have seen Satan with pipes in his belly, out of which come music. I have seen many of these pipes when I have been in intercessory prayer, and they reach all the way up to the sky. As the pipes protrude into the earth, they sing evil songs to one another. They go to people who are vulnerable and whisper things to them such as, "Just kill yourself….Nobody loves you….Nobody cares about you. Just destroy yourself and you'll be a lot better off." These demonic voices sing from one pipe to the other and cause many people to commit suicide because the music and voices that come out of them carry a very ungodly force. It's a seduction to commit suicide...a suicide demon.

Some people have believed false doctrine through demonic influences or erroneous teaching. One time, when I was ministering in Canada, I was sitting in the foyer of the church taking a break. Another woman was sitting there, also, and she said to me, "I've been waiting to talk to you. I've heard that if you kill yourself, you go to heaven. I've been through this and that, and I've planned my death." You wouldn't believe the teachings that people are hearing.

I told her, "That's a lie from the devil. Do you know that if you premeditate, if you decide to kill yourself, you're going to go to hell?" And she said to me, "When I leave here today, I've got it all planned out what I'm going to do." I took her by the hand and said, "Honey, let me pray for you." I began to pray for her and talk to her. The power of God came in, and I counseled her, saying, "You know that if you do this, you'll end up in hell." And she said, "How can that be? I live right, and I do right." I said, "Darling, you're planning your own murder." I prayed and broke that deception by the Holy Spirit. You have to break some things off of people. Later that night, this woman was one of the first to come to the altar to repent of her sins. It's just phenomenal how the Lord will break the hardest heart. We must be on guard against the devil's deception.

Jesus continually used the Word of God to counteract the devil's attacks.

Jesus Himself was tempted by the devil to throw Himself off the pinnacle of the temple. (See Matthew 4:6.)

However, He continually used the Word of God to counteract the devil's attacks:

> *Again, the devil took Him up on an exceedingly high mountain, and showed Him all the kingdoms of the world and their glory. And he said to Him, "All these things I will give You if You will fall down and worship me." Then Jesus said to him, "Away with you, Satan! For it is written, 'You shall worship the LORD your God, and Him only you shall serve.'" Then the devil left Him, and behold, angels came and ministered to Him.* (Matthew 4:8–11)

Jesus was a living example of how to neutralize the devil's attacks: continue to apply the Word of God. Even when it appears as if the devil is continuing to fight against you, you must remain persistent, as Jesus did, until the devil flees from your presence. For every attack that you are currently under, the Word of God has a response. Initially, as you begin to speak the Word, it can seem as if nothing is happening, but remain encouraged. Look at how strongly Jesus stood His ground amid the continued enticements of the devil. The devil is not going to just give up after hearing you speak one Scripture. That is why you must remain persistent and practice due diligence in your active response with the Word of God to slaughter every attack that he uses as an attempt to trick you into giving up. Giving up is not an option.

You have to understand that none of us is beyond the level of being tempted. However, if you heed the wise words of Philippians 2, regardless of what temptations the enemy uses to lure you into self-destruction, you will resist and continue to shine the light of God, even through the darkest moments: "...*children of God without fault in the midst of a crooked and perverse generation, among whom you shine as lights in the world, holding fast the word of life"* (Philippians 2:15–16). You also need to call on strong Christians who can pray for you when you are going through temptation.

Receiving Spiritual Healing

While in hell, I encountered a skeletal form that I could tell was a woman when she spoke. She said to Jesus, "Lord, get me out of hell now! I repent to You. I used to preach Your gospel and I loved Your Bible, but I did not live what I preached." And the Lord said to her, "True." The devil had tempted her husband, and he had committed adultery. When her husband had come back from a trip, he had confessed the infidelity to her and had asked for her forgiveness. However, she had refused to forgive him. He had gone to the church and had tried to get counseling, but she had refused go to the church with him. She had let the devil come into her heart and grow a seed of hatred in her. The Lord explained to her that what her husband had done was truly wrong but that he'd been tempted by the devil. Even though the man had ended the affair, this woman had gotten a gun and killed her husband, the ex-mistress, and herself, but she (the wife) was the only one who had gone to hell.

Whatever is keeping you from receiving salvation through Christ and experiencing a healthy and whole relationship with God, let it go today and ask for forgiveness through the blood of Jesus, and your slate will be as clean as snow. *"Come now, and let us reason together,"* says the LORD, *"though your*

Ask for forgiveness through the blood of Jesus, and your slate will be as clean as snow.

sins are like scarlet, they shall be as white as snow; though they are red like crimson, they shall be as wool" (Isaiah 1:18). Jesus' blood is so powerful that it will wash you clean. Every sin will be blotted out. "*If we walk in the light as He is in the light, we have fellowship with one another, and the blood of Jesus Christ His Son cleanses us from all sin*" (1 John 1:7).

The woman I saw in hell who had once preached the gospel had been living a secret life behind the scenes, but in hell, all hidden deeds are exposed. There are many people like that around us every day. Some have an opportunity to repent of their hidden sinful acts, but others die and go to hell before seeking healing from the toxicity of their hidden lives. God gives us plenty of opportunities to repent that we often ignore. Many of the voices that I heard crying out in hell were weeping with regret. Today, many people have become comfortable with their sin and are still compromising. They don't mean to compromise so carelessly, but they have heard preaching so much and not taken it to heart so that when they finally hear revelation, it sounds foreign to them. Their consciences are hardened and are no longer receptive to the Holy Spirit.

In one of my visions, I saw a coffin with fifteen demons marching around it. There was a man who confessed, "Lord, I ran the preacher out of my room as I was dying." And one woman cried, "I cursed the minister when he came in to pray for me." As they were speaking, the demons would drag them with chains by their feet. The Lord instructed me to listen to them. One of them said, "I didn't think it was wrong to backbite." Then, I looked to the side, and in one corner I saw the heart of hell filled with hypocrites and backbiters. These are people who, because they are led by the lust of the flesh, wind up destroying churches, families, and homes:

> *For the flesh lusts against the Spirit, and the Spirit against the flesh; and these are contrary to one another.* (Galatians 5:17)

A Spiritual Wake-Up Call

We must heed the warning of Scripture and receive spiritual wholeness in this life so that we can have eternal life after we die. Jesus told the story in Luke 16 of a beggar named Lazarus. This man lay begging at a rich man's gate every day. To say that the beggar's health was failing is an understatement. *"The dogs came and licked his sores"* (Luke 16:21). Though the Bible makes no mention of his mental state, we can only imagine the toll it took upon him to sit daily at a gate begging for crumbs. Surely, his destitute situation could only have worsened his already physically debilitated state. After he finally died, however, Lazarus knew no pain or suffering because he had trusted in God.

> *There was a certain rich man who was clothed in purple and fine linen and fared sumptuously every day. But there was a certain beggar named Lazarus, full of sores, who was laid at his gate, desiring to be fed with the crumbs which fell from the rich man's table. Moreover the dogs came and licked his sores. So it was that the beggar died, and was carried by the angels to Abraham's bosom. The rich man also died and was buried. And being in torments in Hades, he lifted up his eyes and saw Abraham afar off, and Lazarus in his bosom.* (Luke 16:19–23)

If you go to hell when you die, you will see clearly everything that you refused to look at or even acknowledge while you lived on the earth. The rich man had refused to look upon the beggar who had sat daily begging at his own gate. Now that the rich man was in hell, however, he *"lifted up his eyes and saw...Lazarus."* This time, the beggar was tucked away safely with Abraham, and the rich man had become the beggar—begging to be loosed from the everlasting torments of hell. *"Many who are first will be last, and the last first"* (Matthew 19:30).

> *Then he* [the rich man] *cried and said, "Father Abraham, have mercy on me, and send Lazarus that he may dip the tip of his finger in water and cool my tongue; for I am tormented in this flame." But Abraham said, "Son, remember that in your lifetime you received your good things, and likewise Lazarus evil things; but now he is comforted and you are tormented. And besides all this, between us and you there is a great gulf fixed, so that those who want to pass from here to you cannot, nor can those from there pass to us."* (Luke 16:24–26)

Some people become so affixed in their sins that they create a gap between themselves and God that seems virtually impossible to bridge. *"They profess to know God, but in works they deny Him, being abominable, disobedient, and disqualified for every good work"* (Titus 1:16). The mind of a person is spiritually sick who professes to know God but whose actions do everything that goes against His Word. Again, the only chance to repair this gap is while we are here upon the earth, and that is only if we will listen to and obey the Word of God. The rich man found this truth out the hard way at the point of no return. Not only could he not save himself, but it was also too late to warn his family:

> *Then he said, "I beg you therefore, father, that you would send him to my father's house, for I have five brothers, that he may testify to them, lest they also come to this place of torment." Abraham said to him, "They have Moses and the prophets; let them hear them." And he said, "No, father Abraham; but if one goes to them from the dead, they will repent." But he said to him, "If they do not hear Moses and the prophets, neither will they be persuaded though one rise from the dead."*   (Luke 16:27–31)

Bridging the Gap

What do you see as the great gulf between you and an opportunity to receive spiritual healing and wholeness? What keeps you from salvation or from renewing a right relationship with God? Is it the riches of this world? An ungodly relationship? Unforgiveness? Whatever the case may be, when you sincerely repent (turn from your own ways and accept God's ways) and become born again, the blood of Jesus' sacrifice on the cross will cleanse you—as if you had never sinned.

> *For the wages of sin is death, but the gift of God is eternal life in Christ Jesus our Lord.* (Romans 6:23)

> *If we say that we have fellowship with Him, and walk in darkness, we lie and do not practice the truth. But if we walk in the light as He is in the light, we have fellowship with one another, and the blood of Jesus Christ His Son cleanses us from all sin. If we say that*

we have no sin, we deceive ourselves, and the truth is not in us. If we confess our sins, He is faithful and just to forgive us our sins and to cleanse us from all unrighteousness. (1 John 1:6–9)

The deception of hell gets us so wrapped up in our problems that we find ourselves operating in the "works of the flesh," doing things that we would not ordinarily do if we were operating in the Spirit:

Now the works of the flesh are evident, which are: adultery, fornication, uncleanness, lewdness, idolatry, sorcery, hatred, contentions, jealousies, outbursts of wrath, selfish ambitions, dissensions, heresies, envy, murders, drunkenness, revelries, and the like; of which I tell you beforehand, just as I also told you in time past, that those who practice such things will not inherit the kingdom of God. But the fruit of the Spirit is love, joy, peace, longsuffering, kindness, goodness, faithfulness, gentleness, self-control. Against such there is no law. And those who are Christ's have crucified the flesh with its passions and desires.
(Galatians 5:19–24)

God is just waiting to show His power through you.

God wants us to know that He loves us and our families, and He wants us to trust Him. He is just waiting to show His power through you. The day I received God's Holy Spirit, everyone was shouting and praising God. The Spirit led me to go to the hospital to pray for a man in intensive care. I went into the room God led me to, and there was a man lying there with an oxygen tent around his bed. I jerked back the oxygen tent and said to him, "You'll go to hell if you die." This was even before God had showed me hell through the revelations.

The man wanted to know the way of salvation, so I led him to the Lord right there. I left the hospital, and a few days later, I got a phone call from this man. He wanted to go with me to church. When we arrived at the church, the pastor allowed the man to tell his testimony.

"Church," he said, "I want to thank God for sending this woman to the hospital to pray for me. I had been in that hospital for 109 days. And I had only minutes to live when she came and showed me the way to salvation." It pays to listen to the Holy Spirit. God sits on the throne. He is a miracle-working God, and He doesn't show partiality. Never refuse to pray for a person just because you don't think he or she is at a level of spirituality that you feel is necessary or deserving of prayer. Your prayer could be the conduit to that person's salvation! Jesus said, *"Those who are well have no need of a physician, but those who are sick. I did not come to call the righteous, but sinners, to repentance"* (Mark 2:17), and *"He [God] makes His sun rise on the evil and on the good, and sends rain on the just and on the unjust"* (Matthew 5:45).

Spiritual Death versus Spiritual Life

In the book of Romans, the apostle Paul set out the contrast and choice between spiritual death and spiritual life:

Those who live according to the flesh set their minds on the things of the flesh, but those who live according to the Spirit, the things of the Spirit. For to be carnally minded is death, but to be spiritually minded is life and peace. Because the carnal mind is enmity against God; for it is not subject to the law of God, nor indeed can be. So then, those who are in the flesh cannot please God. But you are not in the flesh but in the Spirit, if indeed the Spirit of God dwells in you. Now if anyone does not have the Spirit of Christ, he is not His. And if Christ is in you, the body is dead because of sin, but the Spirit is life because of righteousness. But if the Spirit of Him who raised Jesus from the dead dwells in you, He who raised Christ from the dead will also give life to your mortal bodies through His Spirit who dwells in you. (Romans 8:5–11)

Have you received spiritual healing and life through Christ? Whom are you living for? What is the focus of your life? Just as God gave the Israelites a choice, He gives us a choice while we live on this earth:

I have set before you life and death, blessing and cursing; therefore choose life, that both you and your descendants may live; that you may love the Lord *your God, that you may obey His voice, and that you may cling to Him, for He is your life and the length of your days; and that you may dwell in the land which the* Lord *swore to your fathers, to Abraham, Isaac, and Jacob, to give them.* (Deuteronomy 30:19–20)

Chapter 4

HEALING FOR THE SOUL, PART I

"You will keep him in perfect peace, whose mind is stayed on You, because he trusts in You."
—Isaiah 26:3

In addition to spiritual healing, Christ's salvation provides healing for our souls. The soul consists of the mind, will, and emotions; therefore, healing for the soul refers to wholeness in one's thoughts, in one's ability to choose what is right and make wise decisions, and in one's emotional life. The verse above, as well as the following verses, show God's desire to give us peace, comfort, and the assurance of His direction.

> *Trust in the LORD with all your heart, and lean not on your own understanding; in all your ways acknowledge Him, and He shall direct your paths.*
> (Proverbs 3:5–6)

> *To comfort all who mourn, to console those who mourn in Zion, to give them beauty for ashes, the oil of joy for mourning, the garment of praise for the spirit of*

heaviness; that they may be called trees of righteousness, the planting of the LORD, that He may be glorified.
(Isaiah 61:2–3)

For God has not given us a spirit of fear, but of power and of love and of a sound mind. (2 Timothy 1:7)

Is Your Life Burning Out?

Years ago, when I was driving home in my car, I noticed a forest fire roaring about a mile from my house. The fire eventually got as close as the road right outside our home, and my husband yelled, "We have to get everything out of the house! The fire is getting too close." I said, "Oh, no. The devil isn't going to take what God has given to us!" All the neighbors began taking our belongings out of the house, but I stopped them. "Look," I explained, "I believe in the God of miracles, and I believe God can put that fire out. Don't you?" They answered, "We don't know, but we're going to hold hands and pray."

We prayed and bound the devil, and I began to rebuke that fire in the name of Jesus. All the men outside began hollering. It was as if an invisible hand had come down suddenly and pushed that fire into the earth, and it went out! This is not to imply that you should avoid evacuation during a forest fire or another natural catastrophe. Do what God tells you to do. But this incident serves as a reminder that regardless of what situation we are in, we must have faith and know that God has our best interests at heart. Regardless of our circumstances, we have to hold on to the Word of the Lord.

He who dwells in the secret place of the Most High shall abide under the shadow of the Almighty. I will

say of the LORD, "He is my refuge and my fortress;
my God, in Him I will trust." Surely He shall deliver
you from...the perilous pestilence....You shall not be
afraid of the terror by night, nor of the arrow that flies
by day, nor of the pestilence that walks in darkness,
nor of the destruction that lays waste at noonday. A
thousand may fall at your side, and ten thousand at
your right hand; but it shall not come near you.

(Psalm 91:1–3, 5–7)

Sometimes, when those around you are panicking, you must remind them of God's Word. Even if you are afraid, as you apply the Word of God to your situation, He will replace the treacherous infernos of life with focus and peace.

What are you currently facing that is making you feel as if your life is burning out? Whatever it is, give it to God, and He will restore life. Sometimes, life can deal such a treacherous blow that we cannot fathom how we will ever be able to get up and live again. When you are in the fight of your life, there are only two options: (1) fight and persevere until you win, or (2) give up in defeat. Fighting spiritually means declaring to the devil that he cannot have you, your peace, your health, or your family. Whatever the case may be, *"the LORD will give strength to His people; the LORD will bless His people with peace"* (Psalm 29:11).

Emotional Health and Physical Healing

Emotional health, like spiritual wholeness, can lead to physical healing or prevent illness from occurring. Proverbs 18:14 says, *"The spirit of a man will sustain him in sickness, but who can bear a broken ["wounded" KJV] spirit?"* When the spirit of an individual is strong and anchored in the Lord, he or she is more apt to continue fighting for healing. Once the spirit is wounded, however, physical strength may also be negatively affected—and vice versa. When a person has wounded emotions, the desire to maintain physical strength and participate in life can often take a backseat to the inner pain from which the individual is suffering. For someone whose spirit is deeply wounded, a sickness can seem unbearable.

Most of us have been at a place, one time or another, where it seemed as if either physically or mentally we were incapable of going on. Giving up seemed like a much better alternative to continuing to suffer in the same condition. However, something happens within us to spark our will to continue fighting and not give up. Paul wrote that *"God… comforts the downcast"* (2 Corinthians 7:6). Whether it is the encouraging words of a sermon, prayer from friends and loved ones, or reading the Word of God, we are encouraged, comforted, and reminded of the power of faith.

Jesus said, *"If you say to this mountain, 'Be removed and be cast into the sea,' it will be done"* (Matthew 21:21). This astounding revelation of the power of faith is often what leads those who are terminally ill to experience such miraculous results as complete healing. When individuals make up their minds that they are going to believe the Lord with all their hearts and with all their souls, nothing is capable of standing in the way of their healing.

Often, the healthier our souls are, the healthier we are physically.

Often, the healthier our souls are, the healthier we are physically. The Bible gives accounts of men and women whose wounded emotions took a toll on their physical well-being. In the

book of 1 Samuel, we read about Hannah, who was so dis-
tressed over her lack of ability to bear children and of her
rival's provocation that she would not eat.

> Now there was a certain man of Ramathaim Zophim,
> of the mountains of Ephraim, and his name was
> Elkanah....And he had two wives: the name of one
> was Hannah, and the name of the other Peninnah.
> Peninnah had children, but Hannah had no chil-
> dren....And her rival also provoked her severely, to
> make her miserable, because the LORD had closed her
> womb. So it was, year by year, when she went up to
> the house of the LORD, that she provoked her; there-
> fore she wept and did not eat....And she was in bit-
> terness of soul, and prayed to the LORD and wept in
> anguish. Then she made a vow and said, "O LORD of
> hosts, if You will indeed look on the affliction of Your
> maidservant and remember me, and not forget Your
> maidservant, but will give Your maidservant a male
> child, then I will give him to the LORD all the days
> of his life, and no razor shall come upon his head."
> And it happened, as she continued praying before the
> LORD, that Eli [the priest] watched her mouth. Now
> Hannah spoke in her heart; only her lips moved, but
> her voice was not heard. Therefore Eli thought she
> was drunk. So Eli said to her, "How long will you be
> drunk? Put your wine away from you!" And Hannah
> answered and said, "No, my lord, I am a woman of
> sorrowful spirit. I have drunk neither wine nor intoxi-
> cating drink, but have poured out my soul before the
> LORD. Do not consider your maidservant a wicked
> woman, for out of the abundance of my complaint and
> grief I have spoken until now." Then Eli answered and

said, "Go in peace, and the God of Israel grant your petition which you have asked of Him." And she said, "Let your maidservant find favor in your sight." So the woman went her way and ate, and her face was no longer sad. Then they rose early in the morning and worshiped before the LORD, and returned and came to their house at Ramah. And Elkanah knew Hannah his wife, and the LORD remembered her. So it came to pass in the process of time that Hannah conceived and bore a son, and called his name Samuel, saying, "Because I have asked for him from the LORD."
(1 Samuel 1:1–2, 6–7, 10–20)

When Hannah received comfort and peace for her emotions in the promise of God, her countenance changed, and she resumed eating and taking care of herself. She believed the promise of blessing God gave her through Eli, and she received the answer to her prayer.

Healing of Emotional Scars

The heavenly Father wants to heal the wounds and scars of your past. Bishop George Bloomer gives the following account of a spiritual dream he had in which God revealed an emotional wound from his past that he had never fully dealt with.

Waiting for Healing

"I was on a fast, and after about six days of being hungry and frustrated, when time seemed to be slowing down, I remember thinking to myself, *I am getting nowhere.* It dawned on me that I was going on this fast for my church and not for myself. I went to the refrigerator and broke my fast by scooping out several tablespoons of Edy's Butter Pecan Ice Cream and washing them down with cold milk right from the jug. Looking over my shoulders in both directions for something that I could wipe my mouth with, I caught sight of an Entenmann's Crumb Coffee Cake. I reached for the cake, cut a piece, and ate it. Suddenly, I had excruciating abdominal pain. Repenting out loud, I began pleading with God for the pain to subside. I thought that God was punishing me for breaking the fast. Later, however, I learned that the pain was caused by the combination of the ice cream and the ice-cold milk crashing into my stomach, where nothing had been for six days. I went over to the couch, lay down, and fell asleep.

"I had a dream that I was in an emergency room waiting area at a hospital, along with other people. You may think that what I dreamed was inspired by a sugar high or the abdominal pain, but I believe it was a true spiritual dream because of the revelation it gave me. In this waiting room, annoying elevator music was playing over a loudspeaker. When I looked around, I could see what was physically wrong with everyone who was sitting and waiting to be called.

"Some people had lost limbs, while others had lost arms, eyes, or toes. Yet there was nothing wrong with me; I was complete. I thought to myself, *What am I doing here? I'm the only whole person here, and nothing is wrong with me.* There was a man sitting next to me who had lost his right arm, and he was holding the severed arm in his left hand. He looked at me and asked, 'What are you here for?' I replied, 'I don't know.' I returned the question to him: 'Why are you here?' He responded, 'This is the emergency mending place,' and he held up his severed arm and said, 'I'm here to get this sewn back on.'

"Over the loudspeaker, with the elevator music still playing, a woman kept calling out numbers. As she called them, the numbers appeared on the waiting individuals. Everybody had a number except for me. Then I heard her say, 'Number nine,' but no one answered. A woman looked at me and asked, 'Are you going to answer that, or are you going to just keep sitting there? Either answer it or let me go in your place.' I looked at myself and saw the number nine on me. I was number nine!

"I walked to the back, and the atmosphere changed. It was darker, and the music had stopped. I walked past one room where a male doctor was sewing on limbs—an arm, a nose, an ear. I kept walking and saw another man sewing feathers back onto wings that he had pulled out of a box that read, 'This Way Up' and 'Product from Heaven Mills.' Masked nurses were coming in and taking the wings to another physician who was placing the wings back on. When I asked, 'What are you doing?' the doctor replied, 'I'm sewing the feathers back onto the wings of the angels who were injured in battle against satanic forces on our behalf.' Then I went to my doctor and asked, 'What am I doing here? I am the only *whole* person in here. I've lost nothing.' He looked at me and said, 'You're broken, too. You've lost your dad. Your father has been taken from you, but this is the place of mending. The reason why you've been flying so low and haven't been able to catch a high altitude is because of the brokenness.'

"I woke up then, crying frantically, and this dream bothered me for a long, long time. I had needed mending from the age of nine, but I didn't receive it until the age of thirty-two. The Scriptures say, *'Those members of the body which seem to be weaker are necessary. And those members of the body which we think to be less honorable, on these we be-stow greater honor; and our unpresentable parts have greater modesty'* (1 Corinthians 12:22–23). The members of the body that we sometimes disregard because we can't see them are quite significant. Likewise, in my vision, the part of me that needed mending was not visibly represented in the emergency room. I was not aware of my own broken-ness. My concern was, *What am I doing here, seeing that I am whole and they are broken?*

"When my father had been taken from me, it was as if part of me had been lost. In Christ, God had given me per-mission to 'fly high,' spiritually speaking, with no restric-tions. Yet the emotional brokenness I had been experienc-ing for years was causing me to live at a 'lower altitude,' or at diminished spiritual vitality and usefulness.

"After receiving the vision, I ex-pressed to myself the harsh reality of how the loss of my father had affected me. I punched hard at my emotions, and a loud *silence* echoed. It seemed that I was acutely aware of my sur-roundings. I could hear the quiet hum of the refrigerator and movement up-stairs in my house. That type of qui-etness was too noisy for me in my emotional distress. Yet for God to give me a revelation and to take me by the hand and admit me into His hospital was awesome. He gave me the assur-

> *"When I checked out of the 'spiritual ER,' I would 'fly' at an altitude that was prophetically designated for me."*

ance that when I checked out of the 'spiritual ER,' I would, for the first time, 'fly' at an altitude that was prophetically designated for me. That, too, was an incredible thought.

"I am all healed now. However, I still have moments when I daydream and wonder what kind of life I would have had and how wonderful my childhood could have been if I had not lost that 'part' of myself—my father. When we face such natural longings, we can remember these truths:

A father of the fatherless, a defender of widows, is God in His holy habitation. God sets the solitary in families; He brings out those who are bound into prosperity.　　　　　　　　　　　(Psalm 68:5–6)

Blessed be the God and Father of our Lord Jesus Christ, the Father of mercies and God of all comfort, who comforts us in all our tribulation, that we may be able to comfort those who are in any trouble, with the comfort with which we ourselves are comforted by God.　　　　　　　　　　(2 Corinthians 1:3–4)

"The Lord has dealt with me about personal growth and emotional scars in other dreams, as well. Years ago, I kept having a recurring dream in which I'd wake up in the classroom that I had attended as a child. The same teacher was there, and she would ask, 'What brings you to class today?' In the dream, I was grown-up and couldn't even fit my legs underneath the desk. It took me years to realize that God was saying that there were things in my life that I needed to complete.

"For example, when I was writing a book some years ago, God began dealing with me about the little boy who was still living inside my adult frame. I was surprised to learn that with all the obstacles I had already overcome and all the success I'd been allowed to experience, I was still carrying around baggage that was affecting my spiritual growth. I was in need of healing from things in my past—things that ultimately spilled over into my physical and mental well-being.

"God took me through a vision in which He allowed me to see my still-small frame trapped inside my adult-sized body. From that point on, I began seeking Him for complete healing, forgiving those from my past of their wrongdoings, and forgiving myself for the things I'd done to my own life. After going through this process of healing, I felt my ministry catapult to a new level in God, and I felt free from many of the things that had continually plagued me from my past. This healing of the soul played out publicly as people around me began noticing that I'd become much more even-tempered and less agitated and that I received an even greater anointing as I continued preaching the Word of God.

"People can comfort you, but only God can bring ultimate healing."

Allow God to Lead You to Freedom

Many people want to be set free, but they simply do not know where to start. Start with God and allow Him to lead you to the way of freedom. Many who have been in the church for some time have heard statements similar to this so many times that it almost seems like a cliché for them, yet it is a reality: God is a Healer. Even when it seems as if He is not listening, He is. *"I love the LORD, because He has heard my voice and my supplications. Because He has inclined His ear to me, therefore I will call upon Him as long as I live"* (Psalm 116:1–2). God doesn't rush around and become anxious as we do during a crisis, but that does not mean that He isn't concerned with our situations or working on our behalf. *"The Lord is not slack concerning His promise"* (2 Peter 3:9).

> *"For My thoughts are not your thoughts, nor are your ways My ways," says the* LORD. *"For as the heavens are higher than the earth, so are My ways higher than your ways, and My thoughts than your thoughts."*
> (Isaiah 55:8–9)

God does not react to our crises in the same way we react because He already knows the outcomes of them. *"Before they call, I will answer; and while they are still speaking, I will hear"* (Isaiah 65:24).

> *For I am God, and there is no other; I am God, and there is none like Me, declaring the end from the beginning, and from ancient times things that are not yet done, saying, "My counsel shall stand, and I will do all My pleasure."* (Isaiah 46:9–10)

God is concerned about your situation, and He already brought healing to it before it even began to manifest.

Yes, God is concerned about your situation, which is why He already brought healing to it before it even began to manifest. *"By His stripes we **are** healed"* (Isaiah 53:5, emphasis added.) We must have the same perspective.

The devil knows that when we refuse to seek God and to give Him the wounds of the past, it can give demonic strongholds more leverage to continue reminding us of the painful secrets of our past. For instance, studies prove that those suffering from post-traumatic stress disorder (PTSD) feel anxiety, suffer from insomnia, and are easily frightened. The National Institute of Mental Health defines PTSD as "an anxiety disorder that can develop after exposure to a terrifying event or ordeal in which grave physical harm occurred or was threatened."[2] Because the memories of the event are so horrifying, victims suffering from PTSD often avoid anything that could remotely remind them of the traumatizing event. Meanwhile, the devil continues to taunt them with memories of the occasion.

Perhaps your situation is not as traumatizing as to invoke PTSD, but the memories are still so painful that they prevent you from healing and embracing the complete enjoyment of everyday life, as well as service for God. The devil wants you to live within the shadows of your past instead of moving beyond it. God wants you to experience joy in life, not to feel cursed by it. Jesus came to set the captives free. (See Luke 4:18.) Ask God's forgiveness for past failures. And whenever you begin to feel guilt about a situation over which you had no control, you should immediately recognize this as the work of the devil or your own traumatized mind. Release it to God and begin to praise and thank Him for His love and peace.

Continue in faith and in fellowship with God, regardless of what things look like in the natural. The devil will always use your most vulnerable moment to whisper words of defeat, so be alert for his deception and keep your focus steady on God.

You shall be careful to do as the LORD your God has commanded you; you shall not turn aside to the right

---

[2] National Institute of Mental Health. *Post-Traumatic Stress Disorder (PTSD)*, http://www.nimh.nih.gov/health/topics/post-traumatic-stress-disorder-ptsd/index.shtml.

hand or to the left. You shall walk in all the ways which the LORD *your God has commanded you, that you may live and that it may be well with you, and that you may prolong your days in the land which you shall possess.* (Deuteronomy 5:32–33)

Chapter 5

HEALING FOR THE SOUL, PART 2

"He heals the brokenhearted and binds up their wounds."
—Psalm 147:3

Many people struggle with emotions and attitudes—such as fear, anger, grief, and depression—that hinder them from living the life that God desires for them. He wants to release them from these paralyzing emotions so they can fulfill their God-given purposes.

Freedom from Fear

I was ministering at a church in Maryland, and I prayed for a young woman whose mother is a spiritual leader in the church. The young woman immediately wrote down how God had touched her life in many ways that evening, including by encouraging her to let go of her fear and to trust that He is always with her. Here are excerpts from her testimony:

Mary K. Baxter preached at our Virtuous Women's meeting about the importance of prayer. At the end, she gave an altar call for those who wanted an impartation for the anointing for intercession. I was working the altar call as a deacon, monitoring the long line of people waiting to be touched by God. After my line was over, [an elder] asked if I wanted to go up for prayer. I wasn't sure if I needed to get prayed for regarding that particular gift, so I said no. That night, Mary had mentioned that this gift of intercession was not something to take lightly and was not for those who were not willing to sacrifice to pray for others. With this said, I really was not sure if this was a gift I should obtain. Not even a minute later, Mary Baxter and I caught eyes, and she motioned me to the altar.

I stepped in front of Mary and my mother [who was ministering with her], and Mary said she wanted to impart something into my life. Mary laid hands on me and said she saw an angel pouring oil on my head and it covering my body. I could feel the tangible anointing of God all over me, and I began to bend over as the feeling grew stronger. She called for the anointing of intercession—to preach and evangelize. She said God wants to use me greatly and that I would see heaven. I knelt down on the steps, crying and crying and never saying a word. She continued to tell me that God would tell me things at night, some I would not understand, but to write it down, share it with my parents, and ask them for understanding.

[Mary and my mother] both walked away from me and finished praying for the few others at the altar. I continued to kneel there with a tingling sensation all over my body. I'm guessing a few minutes later my mother walked back over to me, sat on the steps in front of me, and laid hands on my head. It felt as if she was pouring the anointing into my very being. It felt like I was about to burst open. I stretched out at this point in an attempt to bear the feeling. It was like my body couldn't hold any more of what she was pouring into me. She began to say many things to me from God. "You never have a need to fear. God is with you wherever you go. He will never leave you. God is always with you. Whatever He asks you to do, you will never do it alone; He will always be with you, working with you; you are never alone," said my mother. I began to cry more just at the thought of how much I've struggled with fear throughout my life and was longing to break free from it. She began to pray in tongues over my life as I was curled up on the floor there crying unto God with moans only God could understand.

Eventually, she let go, and I lay there with my head on the step. It felt as if God was doing brain surgery on my mind....

As I was praying in the Spirit, God began to give me the interpretation of what I was saying. At first, I would try to get it out in English but could not. Eventually, I said, "It is our time!" over and over again. God told me that it was time for the young women to stand up in the things of God. I could picture us as young women walking through the streets as superheroes, fulfilling all that God has called us to do, with signs and wonders to follow....

He also told me that I must pour into the lives of young women and tell them who they are in God....God continued to speak to me, saying, "Don't allow the enemy in your mind, in the gate of your thoughts." I knew I had to guard my heart and mind....

I am so excited about what God has in store for my family in the future. Despite what I see now, I trust God that we all will fulfill our God-given potential.

Healing for our souls involves a renewal of our thoughts and attitudes from negative attitudes so that we can respond to God in love and trust.

"God has not given us a spirit of fear, but of power and of love and of a sound mind" (2 Timothy 1:7). This young woman said that it had felt as if God was doing "brain surgery" on her mind and that she knew she needed to guard her heart and mind from receiving and accepting the lies and deceit of the enemy. Healing for our souls involves a renewal of our thoughts and attitudes from negative attitudes so that we can respond to God in love and trust. The Scriptures say, "Do not be conformed to this world, but be transformed by the renewing of your mind, that you may prove what is that good and acceptable and perfect will of God" (Romans 12:2). We renew our minds by reading, studying, and meditating on God's Word.

Healing of Relationships

One of the areas in which we are most vulnerable to hurt feelings and damaged emotions is in our relationships with family members. In marriage, both partners bring their past emotional wounds—both conscious or unconscious—into the union. Hurts and unresolved issues from the past can prevent them from experiencing healing and reconciliation when conflicts arise between them.

When some people marry, they expect their spouses to remain the same, even thirty to forty years into the marriage. The truth of the matter is, although people stay the same in some ways, they also grow and change as they gain new knowledge and have more life experiences. Sometimes, one spouse changes in a much greater way than the other. This personal growth may be a welcome accentuation to the marriage, but at other times, it can seem like a hindrance. One spouse may seem to "leave behind" the person he or she married, even though they both remain in the same house.

When conflicts related to such changes arise, couples must recognize them for what they are and ask, *What type of change is this? What initiated it? Is it having a positive or negative effect on the marriage, and why?* If we are honest with ourselves, we have to admit that there is always a root cause connected to our reactions to certain behaviors and environments. Our growth, or lack thereof, is related to our experiences in life—the things we go through, our hurts and pains, the good times and bad times, and so forth. The only way to get to the root cause and receive healing is by being completely honest concerning the real issues. Without honesty, we will not really even scratch the surface of the actual problem but will merely waste time.

Some time ago, Bishop Bloomer held a marriage conference in which over half the couples present were experiencing marital crises. Below, he describes how one couple came to understand the underlying cause of their marriage problem.

"One woman asked me why women continue to allow themselves to go through the same thing over and over. To answer her question, I used her own life as an example. She'd shared with me that prior to her current marriage, she'd had two children out of wedlock and had suffered recurring emotional pain from past relationships.

"I said to her, 'You told me that you came from a very good upbringing, with both a mom and dad in the home who taught you great values, right?'

"She answered, 'Yes. Mom never left Dad, and Dad never left Mom; and they're still together today in their eighties.'

"'Okay. So what was your problem?'

"'Well, maybe it was the devil....'

"'But didn't you say that you had two babies out of wedlock? What happened the second time?'

"'Yes, but maybe it was just the devil....He came back stronger.'

"I stopped her again, 'Look, stop lying to yourself and tell the truth. What were you doing?'

"'Well, I was out there, and I was dating, and I know it was wrong, but I got pregnant.'

"'Why?' I asked.

"'Because the enemy was fighting me,' she responded.

"'Tell the truth,' I stopped her the final time. 'You did it because you enjoyed it, and because it felt good to you at the time when you were doing it.'

"'Oh!' she responded, as if understanding this truth for the very first time. Why do you suppose it took her so long to realize this? Because many churches tend to sugarcoat things, sweep them under the carpet, or blame things on the devil that we have control over ourselves. We spend time lying to ourselves and being drawn further into bondage, especially when it comes to such issues as sex—issues that are often too 'taboo' to discuss in religious circles.

"So let's discuss it. Why is sex so good? It's good because God made it, and anytime God makes something, nothing else can be compared to it. Yet when it becomes distorted and manipulated for ungodly use, it becomes the worst type of bondage. Like it or not, that's the truth! When you come together in holy matrimony, it is a blessing, but when you come together outside of marriage, it can become a curse. It is hard for many unmarried couples to break away from it because it's the 'forbidden fruit.' The temptation feeds the desire—and the bondage. When I tell people the truth concerning real issues, they often want to take flight, but deliverance and healing can take place only by first exposing the root cause.

"The same woman whom I'd been addressing then began talking about her husband, who was sitting beside her. 'I pray for my husband all the time because he is so kind, patient, and understanding.'

"I corrected her again. 'No, he isn't. He's not the person you just said he is. What he is, is accommodating. He's accommodating because he doesn't want to ruffle your feathers. So he accommodates your control.'

"She responded, 'Well, I did feel that a few times.'

"'So if you felt that, why didn't you stop it? What you really wanted me to do was to confirm your style of handling him.'

"Their marriage was in desperate need of healing. So I laid hands on them and prayed for them. Before they left to go home, the husband said to me, 'Out of all the conferences, this was the best one I have been to in my life. God really ministered to me.'

"I asked, 'What did God minister to you about?'

"'I thought if I just kept quiet and let her do whatever she wanted to do without saying anything, then it would keep the peace. We live in a nice home and make six figures, but the money is run through like you would not believe. I paid the house off and bought rental properties, and there is more than enough money coming in, but would you believe that we run around every month just trying to find money for gas?' He continued, 'But after today, I'm taking authority.'

"I warned him, 'Don't just "take authority" because I said so. Make sure you're hearing from God.'

"'Oh, no.' he explained. 'It began before we even got to church; that's why we were late. I'd pulled the car to the side of the road and we had a talk. And you confirmed it today.'

"There is no reason for someone making six figures to have to run around scraping for gas money. But God had seen the cry of the husband's heart and had begun His work before I'd even said anything to the two of them during the marriage segment of the conference. I explained to him that he did not need to treat her forcefully or badger her. He only needed to move into a position of healing her. As he was being healed, she, too, needed healing. She was pursuing an image for her life that did not exist, and it was killing her marriage.

"A few days later, the wife called me and confessed, 'Bishop, it's going to be hard, but I know that I have been holding things up in the marriage.' Finally, they were both on the road to healing, but they first had to hear the truth."

A Commitment to Personal Growth

This couple's eyes were opened to the emotional healing they needed for their marriage. Many of us are emotionally unhealthy because we have made a decision *not* to change or have decided to defend our attitudes or actions. Many times, when pastors and evangelists are addressing a congregation as a whole, there is a handful of people who take certain things that are said very personally. For instance, if a pastor is preaching about people who constantly spend money on things they cannot afford, someone will feel as if he or she is being addressed individually. Likewise, if a pastor is speaking on a topic such as abuse or addiction, someone may become offended and follow up with a disgruntled letter or phone call.

We each have a unique combination of experiences. Those who have suffered many emotional wounds in the past may impulsively lash out at those whom they feel are attacking them all over again. Consequently, something that is said in earnest to encourage positive growth of an entire group can be completely misconstrued by those who have deeper wounds than those around them are aware of.

We have to remain committed to continued growth throughout our lives. Always leave room for healing and growth by trusting wholeheartedly in the Lord. Some people go to a garden shop and seek out plants that have already grown, which they can replant. But many people like to plant seeds, instead. Why? They want to be part of the growth process. They patiently wait for the seeds to take root and grow. This is what we must do for the healing of our souls.

Jesus knows the things that we go through on a daily basis. He suffered and died on the cross so that we could cast our cares upon Him, for He cares for us.

> *Humble yourselves under the mighty hand of God, that He may exalt you in due time, casting all your care upon Him, for He cares for you. Be sober, be vigilant; because your adversary the devil walks about like a roaring lion, seeking whom he may devour. Resist him, steadfast in the faith, knowing that the same sufferings are experienced by your brotherhood in the world. But may the God of all grace, who called us to His eternal glory by Christ Jesus, after you have suffered a while, perfect, establish, strengthen, and settle you.*
>
> (1 Peter 5:6–10)

Jesus wants you to know today that He hears your prayers and that there is nothing too hard for Him.

When we are weak, God sends His Spirit and His angels to make us strong. Even when Jesus got a glimpse of how gruesome His death would be, He still insisted, *"Not My will, but Yours, be done"* (Luke 22:42). Surely, Jesus would not have gone through all of that just for us to continue suffering in emotional pain as those who are without any hope. There *is* hope, and His name is Jesus—the One who died for us so that we might be set free from the curses of sin and death. Jesus wants you to know today that He hears your prayers and that there is nothing too hard for Him. (See Isaiah 59:1.)

Healing from Grief

One of the most difficult emotions or states of mind for many to overcome is grief. When my son died, I decided to cancel all my appointments and stay home, but then I heard the voice of the Lord say to me, "You can either stay home and cry, or go win souls and heal the sick for Me." I decided to keep my appointments, and, after I'd fallen asleep, I had a vision of my son confirming that I'd made the right decision. Going through a period of grief is a normal process in dealing with the loss of someone whom we love and cherish dearly, and we must understand that each person grieves in his or her own way.

The devil does not always know the plan of God for our lives, but he does know that as children of God, we hold the power to release the angels of the Lord to do His will as we exercise faith and pray. The enemy therefore tries to keep us in a state of grief for long periods of time because he knows that in that state, no intercession will go on. When intercession stops, the work of God on our behalf is hindered. It is to the enemy's benefit to keep us in a posture of mourning instead of in a posture of warfare. I believe that when intercession stops, angels stop moving. Opportunities are lost because many Christians are too easily manipulated through their emotions. That is why diligence to the enemy's tactics is so important.

Removing Resistance to Healing

Again, it is natural for us to feel the loss and pain of a void that was once filled by someone whom we held dear. Jesus Himself grieved deeply at the death of Lazarus. By the time Jesus reached Lazarus, his tomb had been sealed, for Lazarus had been dead for four days. Still, Jesus demanded that they take away the stone. (See John 11:17–44.)

For us, it is not a physical stone that blocks our spiritual resurrection but a mental stone that hinders us from continuing in life after the reality sets in that our loved one is gone. We put up a wall that prevents us from even acknowledging the fact that death has taken place; consequently, we may spend the rest of our lives stagnated at the point of death. Even when we don't realize it, our minds and emotions remain at the places where our loved ones lie. We go through the motions of living, but we are as the walking dead. The walls that we put up prevent us from even discussing such sensitive issues as death. We tiptoe around the fact that someone has actually died instead of acknowledging how we really feel.

However, just as Jesus demanded the physical removal of the stone from Lazarus's tomb, we can order, in Jesus' name, that the stone keeping us from going through the grieving process be removed so that healing may take place in our lives. Acknowledging sadness is not a sign of weakness; rather, it is the beginning of healing.

Jesus was not dissuaded by Lazarus's death but insisted, *"Did I not say to you that if you would believe you would see the glory of God?"* (John 11:40). When will you allow the glory of God to again be fulfilled in your life? How would your loved ones feel if they knew that when they died, you died along with them? Would they not be grieved? Would they not demand that you allow them to live eternally in peace with God as you continue to live out your life peaceably upon the earth, acknowledging that Jesus promised, *"I am the resurrection and the life"* (verse 25) and that they will rise again? Find solace by keeping your mind focused on another of Jesus' promises: *"Blessed are those who mourn, for they shall be comforted"* (Matthew 5:4). We read in the psalms, *"He heals the brokenhearted and binds up their wounds"* (Psalm 147:3).

There is no replacement for the loved ones whom we miss so dearly. However, if we keep our faith in God and continue to remain true to Him, the grief will become much more bearable, and God will sustain us.

Bringing Healing to Others Who Grieve

A Comforting Presence

God desires that we comfort others in their grief, as He has comforted us. *"That we may be able to comfort those who are in any trouble, with the comfort with which we ourselves are comforted by God"* (2 Corinthians 1:4). We can help others to find healing from grief by ministering to them with sensitive hearts. We should follow Jesus' example and comfort others with the Word of God or simply let them know that we will be part of a support system for them in their time of need.

Words cannot always bring comfort at such times, but just knowing that someone is there with them can bring people great solace. The worst thing that could happen is for grieving persons to continually be surrounded by influences that distress them even further. This was Job's

The best way to assist a person who is in mourning is often just to provide him or her with your presence.

experience when the one closest to him—his wife—demanded, after they had lost all their children and everything they owned, "*Do you still hold fast to your integrity? Curse God and die!*" (Job 2:9). Cursing God was the last thing that Job needed to do in the midst of his crisis. Again, the best way to assist a person who is in mourning is often just to provide him or her with your presence. When Job's friends first heard of his loss, they stopped what they were doing and immediately went to Job's side.

> *Now when Job's three friends heard of all this adversity that had come upon him, each one came from his own place; Eliphaz the Temanite, Bildad the Shuhite, and Zophar the Naamathite. For they had made an appointment together to come and mourn with him, and to comfort him. And when they raised their eyes from afar, and did not recognize him, they lifted their voices and wept; and each one tore his robe and sprinkled dust on his head toward heaven. So they sat down with him on the ground seven days and seven nights, and no one spoke a word to him, for they saw that his grief was very great.* (Job 2:11–13)

Negative influences during grief can take the form of demonic spirits who attack with tormenting thoughts or human beings who spew negativity rather than speak words of encouragement. This is what eventually happened to Job. Initially, Job's three friends had the best of intentions, but their presence later became a burden to Job. They began aggravating his wounds instead of soothing them. They accused him of sin, yet they could not offer any proof that he had sinned in the ways in which they accused him. This infuriated Job's friend Elihu: *"Against his three friends his wrath was aroused, because they had found no answer, and yet had condemned Job"* (Job 32:3). Job did not need those around him pointing out his supposed sins against God or failing to show him the root cause of God's eventual discontentment with him. Job was not without guilt, and God was angry with Job for how he was responding to the tragedies in his life.

God asked Job, *"Shall the one who contends with the Almighty correct Him? He who rebukes God, let him answer it"* (Job 40:2). And Job responded, *"Behold, I am vile; what shall I answer You? I lay my hand over my mouth"* (verse 4). Later, God continued His rebuke by reprimanding Job's friends:

> *And so it was, after the LORD had spoken these words to Job, that the LORD said to Eliphaz the Temanite, "My wrath is aroused against you and your two friends, for you have not spoken of Me what is right, as My servant Job has. Now therefore, take for yourselves seven bulls and seven rams, go to My servant Job, and offer up for yourselves a burnt offering; and My servant Job shall pray for you. For I will accept him, lest I deal with you according to your folly; because you have not spoken of Me what is right, as My servant Job has."* (Job 42:7–8)

Again, the last thing a grieving individual needs is someone around him or her relaying "God's thoughts" regarding that individual's tragedy, especially when the person is giving a wrong interpretation. We must let the person who has experienced loss express sorrow and work through it. Never encourage a grieving person to withhold tears—remember, Jesus Himself wept at the news of His friend Lazarus's death. There is a time to mourn, and our tears are so significant to God that He keeps a record of them. *"Put my tears into Your bottle; are they not in Your book?"* (Psalm 56:8). I believe that God had kept a precise record of every tear that Job had shed for his losses, and He *"blessed the latter days of Job more than his beginning"* (Job 42:12).

Sensitivity to Coping with Loss

We sometimes rush to judge the methods others use to cope with a loss. Instead, we should allow them to grieve in their own ways as they lean on God. Depending on the circumstance, David grieved for people in different ways. When David's son died, his servants questioned the way he conducted himself.

> *When David saw that his servants were whispering, David perceived that the child was dead. Therefore David said to his servants, "Is the child dead?" And they said, "He is dead." So David arose from the ground, washed and anointed himself, and changed his clothes; and he went into the house of the LORD and worshiped. Then he went to his own house; and when he requested, they set food before him, and he ate. Then his servants said to him, "What is this that you have done? You fasted and wept for the child while he was alive, but when the child died, you arose and ate food."* (2 Samuel 12:19–21)

The servants failed to understand that this was David's way of letting go in order to live. He responded to them,

While the child was alive, I fasted and wept; for I said, "Who can tell whether the LORD will be gracious to me, that the child may live?" But now he is dead; why should I fast? Can I bring him back again? I shall go to him, but he shall not return to me."

(verses 22–23)

To the servants, David's grieving seemed to be a backward process. They failed to realize that David found solace in the fact that although his son would never return to him on the earth, David would see him again in heaven.

On another occasion, David mourned the death of King Saul, as well as Jonathan, who was the king's son and David's best friend:

David took hold of his own clothes and tore them, and so did all the men who were with him. And they mourned and wept and fasted until evening for Saul and for Jonathan his son, for the people of the LORD and for the house of Israel, because they had fallen by the sword.   (2 Samuel 1:11–12)

While David had known that his son might die, the deaths of Saul and Jonathan were relatively sudden and took David by surprise. The heartbreaking toll of one occasion of death was no greater than another occasion. Only the methods by which David grieved differed. There are no hard-and-fast rules regarding how one person must grieve. Each deals with his or her own unique experience and the pain attached to it.

In 2 Samuel 3, David mourned the death of Abner, the commander of Saul's army, who was killed by the sword at the hands of David's general Joab and his brother Abishai.

Again, David tore his clothes and mourned in sackcloth and ashes. He followed behind the coffin and accompanied Abner's body to bid one last farewell at his burial. When the people attempted to persuade David to eat, he refused, saying, *"God do so to me, and more also, if I taste bread or anything else till the sun goes down!"* (2 Samuel 3:35).

Each time, David mourned according to the situation that had led up to the death. This time, he not only mourned Abner's death, but he also mourned the way in which he had died: *"Should Abner die as a fool dies? Your hands were not bound nor your feet put into fetters; as a man falls before wicked men, so you fell"* (verses 33–34). To David, Abner's death was an unnecessary and wasteful tragedy.

Many times, people find great solace in the fact that their loved ones died doing things in which they took great pride. It is what many widows and widowers of fallen soldiers relate to when their spouses are killed in battle. Those looking from the outside in do not always understand this way of thinking, but it corresponds to the teaching of Philippians 4:8, which says, *"If there is any virtue and if there is anything praiseworthy; meditate on these things."*

In times of sorrow, remembering the positive aspects of a person's life can bring some solace, even in the midst of the pain. Initially, this can be a struggle because the void is overwhelming and may block any positive thoughts. As time progresses, however, people find that the memories of life are a soothing reminder of the precious moments they were able to share with a person whom they will always hold dear to their hearts. This is what drives some individuals to create scholarships in memory of loved ones, or to remember them in memorial services, and so forth. Remember that each person has his or her own unique way of dealing with the loss of loved ones and that the process by which that person uses to heal is just as unique.

Healing from Depression

Sometimes, people cross a line from a healthy grieving process to deep depression. The one who is still alive can die mentally and emotionally if he or she does not find relief. In the following passage, Bishop Bloomer describes his battle against depression after the death of his brother.

"Years ago, when my brother died, the experience was very difficult for me to cope with. He'd lived a rough life, and to see him lying there in his coffin only fueled the pain and grief that I was already feeling prior to arriving at his funeral. I found myself simply and quietly going through the motions. Although I was physically present, I had checked out mentally and emotionally; yet, I was able to hide the true depth of my turmoil from those who were around me.

"It was as if I were in a dream—walking, talking, seeing, hearing, and touching but not feeling a thing. I watched as the funeral directors mouthed their final words and began to shut his coffin. As they shut it, I remember hearing a loud "click," at which point, inwardly, I lost it. No one knew that I had snapped because I immediately went to my car and began driving alone. As I drove over the Verrazano Bridge in New York, I could feel a demonic influence in the car trying to convince me to drive off the bridge. The more I drove, the louder the voice became. As I wept, I began silently calling upon the name of Jesus. I will never forget what happened next. The atmosphere in the car suddenly began to change. A peace overtook me unlike any that I'd experienced before. The presence in the car was so strong that I shot my eyes to the passenger seat to make sure I was alone. As I glanced to my right, an indentation formed in the seat, as if an invisible force was sitting right beside me. I could see no one, but I could feel the presence of someone else in the car. It was as if time stood still, and I allowed the peace of God to take over my entire being. I turned the car around and headed back to join my family members, who was still gathered together.

"A peace overtook me unlike any that I'd experienced before."

"God 'will not allow you to be tempted beyond what you are able, but with the temptation will also make the way of escape, that you may be able to bear it' (1 Corinthians 10:13). I am convinced that on that day, the ungodly temptation to take my own life was unbearable, and as I called upon the name of the Lord, His intervention kept me from making a decision that would have been tragic, not only for myself but for my family, as well."

It is important for those undergoing grief and for those desiring to support them to be able to discern the difference between a healthy grieving process that leads to healing and a destructive depression from which a person may find it nearly impossible to escape without intervention. The American Psychiatric Association notes,

Sadness and depression are not the same. While feelings of sadness will lessen with time, the disorder of depression can continue for months, even years. Patients who have experienced depression note marked differences between normal sadness and the disabling weight of clinical depression.[3]

Although the symptoms of depression can vary, some of the signs are as follows:

+ Loss of interest in normal daily activities
+ Problems sleeping
+ Trouble focusing or concentrating
+ Irritability
+ Feeling fatigued or weak
+ Feeling worthless
+ Thoughts of suicide or suicidal behavior[4]

First Peter 5:7 urges us to cast our cares upon the Lord because He cares for us. Conversely, our *"adversary the devil walks about like a roaring lion, seeking whom he may devour"* (verse 8). The devil uses our most vulnerable moments to wreak even more havoc in our lives. Don't fall for his deceptive tactics. Recognize the difference between sadness and depression and be prepared to ward off the devastating effects of despair. Initially, it can seem as if the grief will never fade. As you determine to continue persevering and keep your mind focused on the things of God, however, you will find the loss easier to bear. But if you give up, you will never realize how close you were to victory or to living the life that your loved one would have wanted you to see fulfilled.

---

[3] *Let's Talk Facts about Depression*, American Psychiatric Association (2005), http://www.healthyminds.org/Document-Library/Brochure-Library/Lets-Talk-Facts-Depression.aspx.
[4] Mayo Clinic, http://www.mayoclinic.com/health/depression/DS00175/DSECTION=symptoms.

During difficult times, make sure that you are around people who can encourage you and strengthen you in the Lord. Do not stay by yourself too long or allow your thoughts to go in a despairing direction. Jesus said, *"Peace I leave with you, My peace I give to you; not as the world gives do I give to you. Let not your heart be troubled, neither let it be afraid"* (John 14:27). Remember also these words:

> *Be anxious for nothing, but in everything by prayer and supplication, with thanksgiving, let your requests be made known to God; and the peace of God, which surpasses all understanding, will guard your hearts and minds through Christ Jesus. Finally, brethren, whatever things are true, whatever things are noble, whatever things are just, whatever things are pure, whatever things are lovely, whatever things are of good report, if there is any virtue and if there is anything praiseworthy; meditate on these things.*
>
> (Philippians 4:6–8)

Finally, for those of us who minister to others who are grieving, the Scripture urges us to *"love one another fervently with a pure heart"* (1 Peter 1:22) and to *"bear one another's burdens, and so fulfill the law of Christ"* (Galatians 6:2).

Chapter 6

HEALING FOR THE BODY

"Beloved, I pray that you may prosper in all things and be in
health, just as your soul prospers."
—3 John 1:2

Salvation through Jesus provides us first with healing for our spirits—a new nature, a right relationship with our heavenly Father, and eternal life. Second, it enables us to receive healing for our minds and emotions so that we can be at peace in the midst of life's trials, reflect God's character, and make decisions in line with His Word. Third, it enables us to receive physical healing. *"By His stripes we are healed"* (Isaiah 53:5).

An Outpouring of Grace

God has extended many great mercies to me throughout my life. When I reach a point of despair, He always responds with an outpouring of grace. *"From the fullness of his [Jesus'] grace we have all received one blessing after another"* (John 1:16 NIV), and one of those blessings is physical healing.

Once, when I was at home praying, I sensed that something was wrong with one of my children. Sure enough, my son came stumbling through the patio door and collapsed right in front of me! His friends explained that he had been playing football and one of the larger players had accidentally stepped on his head. I immediately called his father at work. He came home, and the two of us rushed our son to the hospital as he was falling into unconsciousness. On the way to the hospital, the car's engine blew up, and by the time we finally got to the hospital, all I could do was cry. I couldn't pray or do anything else.

Some fellow Christians came to the hospital and explained to me that I had lost my faith. Yet, throughout my son's life, he'd been attacked in his head. I was just so tired of the devil attacking my son in this way. On a previous occasion, he'd been ill and we had rushed him to the hospital, where he'd been diagnosed as epileptic.

So, this particular episode, during which his little body had collapsed in front of me, seemed just too much for me. In my desperation, I cried out, *Just take him, God!* After undergoing numerous tests and staying at the hospital all evening, my son regained consciousness. All tests appeared normal, and he was released from the hospital after midnight. Thank the Lord! When we got home, my husband agreed to stay up and watch our son while I went to bed. I went into the bathroom, and the peace of God seemed to overtake me all at once. I got on my knees, and God opened my mouth. Instantly, I thought, *I'm really going to get it from God now because of what I said in that hospital* (telling Him to just take my son). However, it wasn't God's intention to "get me." It was His intention to comfort and heal me.

Weeks earlier, I had gone to the dentist, and as the dentist was working on my teeth, the drill had slipped and flown across the room, so they had left one of my teeth with just a cotton pack in it. I had told my husband, "If God doesn't fill my teeth, then they won't be filled." Well, I had forgotten all about that statement, but God had not forgotten it. He began to fill my teeth in the bathroom after we'd brought my son home from the hospital.

Not once did He rebuke me for telling Him to take my son. Instead, He healed me by filling my teeth! When I finally looked at the clock, I noticed that it was four o'clock in the morning. God had worked on my mouth for four hours. I ran down the hallway and cried out to my husband, "Look, look, God filled my teeth!" He didn't believe it and just told me to go to bed. So, the next morning, I showed him the miracle that God had performed!

As I've ministered the gospel in the United States and overseas, I have encountered this miracle of God many times. He fills people's teeth in order to show them His power. One time, a friend of mine came to my house. She had heard that God was filling teeth in the church services, and she said, "I've got a bad tooth, and I want God to fill it." I said, "Well, I can't guarantee you that God will fill your teeth; it's not me, it's God. I'll pray for you and anoint you, but it has to be God." That night, she actually opened up her mouth like a baby bird, believing that God could fix her tooth. This is faith. She really believed God. The next morning, her tooth was fixed with what looked like white pearl. She told people in various church services that God had fixed her

God fills people's teeth in order to show them His power.

tooth, and when she did, other people's teeth were filled, also. That happens a lot when people get up and testify.

I was preaching at Hudson Bay, Canada, and a lady came up who had about ten cavities. I prayed with her, and she fell on the floor and began to roll, cry, and scream. I thought, *Well, God, I wonder what happened to her?* Later, she got up and came back to me and said, "Look at my mouth." God had filled all her teeth with gold. She explained, "I was shouting with joy and crying because there was no pain at all. I knew what He was doing." I said, "Well, you need to tell people." Yet this woman didn't give her testimony for three years. Then, she came to where I was ministering, and I made her come up and tell the congregation. Many people's teeth were repaired that night because she told what the Lord had done for her.

My mother-in-law had a church in Pennsylvania, and one day, we were praying for people's teeth there. We both saw, in a vision, streams of gold that were about two inches wide. These tiny widths of gold went down and lay in people's teeth where there were cavities, and the angels fixed the people's teeth.

God was showing His power, and it was amazing because one of the people He healed there did not seem to be living for Him and was a hypocrite. But God is merciful.

On another occasion, I was ministering at a church in New York. A woman whose teeth were giving her trouble was the first one to come up to be prayed for that night, and I prayed for her. The next morning, toward the end of the church service, she said, "I have a testimony." I asked her what it was, and she said, "You remember the other night when I couldn't eat because my mouth was hurting too bad? Well, look!" She opened her mouth to reveal the most beautiful fillings. She explained, "I couldn't afford to go to the dentist, and God filled my teeth."

When I was in Malaysia to minister, I met a pastor's wife who asked, "Can you pray for me, because I have a lot of holes in my teeth?" So I placed my hands on her face, and for a while, I could not remove my hands. When I finally finished praying and removed my hands from her face, the holes in her teeth were filled with gold. When God gets ready to show Himself, He does it regardless of what others might think. You have to learn to discern the voice of God because, again, His ways are not our ways, and His thoughts are not our thoughts.

Another time, I was ministering to about two hundred people in another nation, and I talked about God's miraculous power to fix people's teeth. There was a baby there who was about a year and a half old and was still on milk. The mother had the baby in her arms, and the baby was crying. The child had tiny teeth in front, but some of them were decayed and falling out. The mother said, "The dentist can't do anything." My heart went out to that baby because there's nothing worse than a toothache! I went over and laid hands on the baby, and then I went on down the prayer line. I had prayed for about fifteen other children when the mother screamed. God had healed and regrown all those teeth within fifteen minutes. That was a miracle! Then, many more children's teeth were fixed that day. Little babies don't know what faith is, but children are healed through the love and power of the Lord as we pray for them.

Children are healed through the love and power of the Lord as we pray for them.

Others have also experienced the healing of their teeth. My friend Pastor Harry Sauer of Faith Fire Word Center in Titusville, Florida, testified,

> Mary K. Baxter prayed for my teeth, and I received a gold crown on my left bottom molar. When I went back to the dentist, he asked me what happened because he did not put the crown there. They don't use that quality of gold. I told him I got prayed for and Jesus healed and filled my tooth, praise God!

Another pastor from Independence, Missouri, wrote,

> When Sister Baxter came to our church, I had no idea I would receive fillings in my teeth. I had been going to the St. Elizabeth clinic for a few months now for X-rays, cleanings, and extracts. Because they are so busy, my appointments are one to two months apart....But that night, when she called out, 'Someone, or there's two of you that have to get fillings, three or four for your teeth,' I stood right up; through obedience from the Holy Spirit, I went up to the sanctuary to the sister—and got my silver fillings. I thought I got three, but when I got home, there were three on the left bottom and one on the left top!...What this means to me, though, is that we do definitely serve the same God that raised Lazarus from the dead, the same God that parted the Red Sea when He saved the Israelites,... the God that did a miracle for my daughter and kept her alive....

Twelve Major Miracles

We should never doubt the power of God. On one occasion, my spiritual daughter and I went to a church where the music was so loud that she decided to sit in the back row because her ears were very sensitive. Out of the side door came twelve angels with a long table, and they had twelve transparent boxes with locks on them. I prayed, *Jesus, what's this?* and He replied, *There are going to be twelve major miracles here this morning.* He continued, *Look at the first box.* Locked in the box was a beating heart. The next box held yellow sponges inside it. I thought to myself, *What in the world is that?* The Spirit said, *There are people in here with asthma, and we're going to touch them with these* [items inside the box] *and heal them of their asthma.* There was a kneecap in one box, a nerve in another, and so forth.

I became so overwhelmed that I asked God, *Lord, how am I going to do all this?* So, I called my spiritual daughter from the back of the church to meet me in the corner, and I asked her what she saw. She was a bit hesitant to share it with me at first, but then she went on to describe the same things I'd seen in my vision!

When I stood before the people, the first thing I asked was, "Is there anyone in here who needs healing from asthma or who has bad lungs from smoking?" Immediately, people jumped up and came to the front of the church, and the angels of the Lord took a key, opened that box, and ran over and began touching their lungs. These people fell down on the floor under the power of God and arose healed. One of them even testified, "I saw an angel with a funny object in its hand. I'm embarrassed to tell you what it looked like, but it looked like a sponge." That was yet another confirmation of the vision my daughter and I had seen earlier.

In a moment, God had removed her illness and made her as brand-new.

Then, we found out that the pastor of the church needed a heart and that she always walked with a limp from a bad knee. During this service, she, also, fell down under the Spirit of God, and the wings of an angel began to cover her. When she finally got up off the floor, she went to her office weeping. Later, she visited her doctor and called afterward to give us the report. Her heart was brand-new, and her leg was completely healed. She was a young pastor, and the devil had created all this illness in her life, but in a moment, God had removed it and made her as brand-new.

Healing from Demonic Attack

Once, I went to Taiwan to minister for a month, and we held big conventions where there were interpreters. One night, a woman came into the church with her two-year-old daughter in a stroller. The child could not hold her head up, and she was small for her age. An angel of the Lord was there, and he showed me a vision of this child. I don't want to disturb any who are mothers with what I say next. This may be difficult to receive, but it is important to be aware of the attacks that the enemy may wage against children. In this vision, I saw a small black serpent wrapped around that child's neck. I could see it as if I were looking at a television screen.

They brought the child up to the front row in a stroller, and the mother was sitting there praising God. The Holy Spirit said to me, *They won't be able to interpret what I'm saying. I want you to go down and lay hands on that baby.* So,

I told the man there, and I went down and laid hands on the child and prayed and touched her neck. In the Spirit, I saw an angel of the Lord pull that snake off. When he did, the child's head was flopping. Then, the Lord said, *Now you must pray for strength in the neck.* The child had had this problem since birth, and she was now two years old. He said, *I will strengthen that baby's neck and head.* I prayed and prayed for the child and anointed her with oil. Before the service was over, the mother began jumping up and shouting because she noticed that the child began to look better and had started to be able to hold her little head up.

Backs Restored

These miracles just thrill my soul. I have seen all kinds of healings, including the healing of many back problems. I have prayed for people whose legs have grown out two or three inches. One man had not bent over in twenty years. We prayed, and Jesus healed his back.

A man named Ed wrote to me,

You prayed for my lower back, and yesterday and today I have been almost 100 percent pain free. I have been healed with the blood of Jesus. I swam in the pool today and had a great day. I praised Him all day and thanked Him for blessing me and healing my back.

Bishop Bloomer gives the following account of when his mother was healed of severe back pain after doubting God's healing power.

"I was introduced to healing by my mother. Well-known faith healers of the twentieth century, such as Oral

Roberts, A. A. Allen, and Kathryn Kuhlman, had a great influence on her. She had pictures and magazine and newspaper clippings about their services, which she cherished.

"Yet before this, for quite some time, she had suffered from a bad back condition. Though it's not clear to me where or when she was injured, I know that when I was growing up, she had excruciating pain and complained of her back hurting all the time.

"One evening, when I came home, she was sitting in front of the television, crying. I asked her what was wrong, and she told me that her back was on fire. 'Ma,' I asked, 'are you hurting? Do we need to call the doctor?' She began to explain, 'No. This is a good fire. It's like liniment.' Liniment was an awful, minty-smelling ointment that people used to rub on their backs and muscles to alleviate pain—similar to Aspercreme today. She continued, 'I feel like a heating pad is pressed against my spine, and it feels so good.' Then, pointing at the television screen, she said, 'I think that lady right there—look at her, George—has healed me.' I looked, and 'that lady' to whom my mother was referring was Kathryn Kuhlman.

"I was really amazed by my mother's statement because she had previously spent so much time trying to disprove miraculous healings, saying that they were something of the past. She would even thumb her nose at modern medicines and instead resort to using alternative treatments, such as herbs and exercises, to alleviate her pain, though to no avail. On that wonderful Saturday night, however, my mother received her healing, her miracle. Had it been any other night, my mother probably would not have seen Kathryn Kuhlman. You see, my mother was a Seventh-day Adventist, and they keep the Sabbath on Saturday. Had it been any other day, she would not have been watching Christian television. Had it been any other night, Kathryn Kuhlman would not have been on television, but God used her as a vessel to heal my mother. He did not use Kathryn Kuhlman simply for the physical healing of my mother's chronic pain, but more important, to reveal Himself to her in the Person of the Lord Jesus Christ.

"I, too, would go on to experience healings. Many times in my life, I have seen God's miraculous healing power. When I was a youth, I was strung out on drugs, and my heart actually stopped one night from a near-fatal drug overdose. Except by the grace of God, and through my mother's prayers, I would have died in the emergency room. But God had other plans for my life. God is real, and His power is evident."

Raised from the Dead!

Yes, God raises the dead, even in our day. I was preaching at a service in Illinois some years ago, and there was a woman sitting in the front row looking as stiff as a board. God revealed to me that she'd just died, so I went to her husband and whispered, "I think your wife has died." He replied, "Oh, she always looks like that." Even under the circumstances, it was funny to hear him say that, but I still insisted, "No, she's dead. God just revealed to me that she has died." So, we called 9-1-1, and when the paramedics came, she did not have a pulse. They placed her on a gurney, and, as they were rolling her out, she sat up. I looked over at her husband, who again said, "I told you, she always looks like that." In my heart, I knew that God had raised her from the dead. We later found out that she was diabetic and had taken too much insulin before the service and overdosed on it.

> *"When God is revealing something to me, I must have faith and obey because someone's life could depend upon how I react."*

I have learned that when God is revealing something to me, I must have faith and obey because someone's life could depend upon how I react.

Another time, I was at my mother-in-law's church and was sitting beside an elderly woman whose nephew was preaching. She suddenly began sliding down in the chair. *Oh no*, I thought to myself. *If this woman dies in my mother-in-law's church, everyone is going to talk about it.* She just kept stiffening up and sliding down in the chair. I tried whispering to her nephew, but he couldn't hear me. Finally, I yelled up to the pulpit, "Your aunt has died!"

He jumped down and began giving her mouth-to-mouth resuscitation. When he did that, the most foul odor filled the entire sanctuary. It was unlike any smell I had ever experienced before. While we were waiting for the paramedics to come, I said to her nephew and my mother-in-law, "We have to pray for God to raise this woman from the dead because surely she is not ready to go meet the Lord!"

When the paramedics arrived, they couldn't get a pulse. As they were putting her on the gurney, I just could not let go of the fact that this woman, although she was ninety-something years old, was not ready to meet the Lord. I insisted, "Her soul is not right with God.

We've got to remit her sins and give her life to God." So we continued to pray, and as they were rolling her out on the gurney, her hand moved. I rushed over to her and immediately asked, "Are you saved? If not, you need to get saved right now and give your life to God." We went through the sinner's prayer with her, and she got off the gurney. She said to us, "Do you know what I saw when I died? My soul came out of my body and I floated across this room and watched all of you as you prayed for me and gave me mouth-to-mouth resuscitation. When you were praying to God for my soul to go back into my body, it's like I had no control over it. It just went right back into my body." This is proof of just one of the many things that God can do.

From the cradle to the grave, God is with us. Whether you believe it or not, sometimes people lying on their death-beds are those to whom God's grace is being extended because He wants to give them time to get their lives right with Him. We have to learn to take dominion over death. When we pray in the Holy Spirit, He knows the perfect prayer for us to pray over a dying person.

You have to have faith in whatever area of ministry God calls you to because it is meant to serve the needs of others.

> *The manifestation of the Spirit is given to each one for the profit of all: for to one is given the word of wisdom through the Spirit, to another the word of knowledge through the same Spirit, to another faith by the same Spirit, to another gifts of healings by the same Spirit, to another the working of miracles.*
> (1 Corinthians 12:7–10)

You must begin to claim a miracle, regardless of what it looks like in the natural.

If you have cancer or some other ailment that is terminal, you must begin to claim a miracle, regardless of what it looks like in the natural. One time, when I was traveling overseas, I became very sick. I was so weak that I could barely move. I immediately began rebuking the devil because he was trying to fill my mind with all types of evil reports when I hadn't even been to the doctor to get a diagnosis. When you begin to curse the works of darkness, angels begin to work.

I made up my mind that I was going to the doctor. The doctors gave me an MRI and could not find anything wrong with me. Still, I was still so sick that I could barely hold up my head. Six weeks went by. Then, one night, I had a dream in which I saw Jesus on the cross. I saw Him being pierced in the side, and then He spoke to me in the dream and said, "By My stripes, you are healed." He began to explain to me, "Child, you have a fungus in your lungs, and you have to curse it in My name and I will heal you." So, I began doing that in the dream. I cursed the sickness in Jesus' name and put my trust in Him to heal me. I awoke the next morning with energy that I had not experienced in a very long time. All the weakness was completely gone!

Questions about Physical Healing

Many people have questions about physical healing when they deal with sickness and disease, and to conclude this chapter, I would like to address some of these concerns.

1. *Should we use doctors and medicine, or should we just pray?*

I believe that God does work in conjunction with doctors. There are many Holy Spirit-filled doctors and nurses today. Luke, the author of the gospel of Luke and the book of Acts, was a physician. In addition, many lives have been saved through medicine. People who don't know the Lord go to doctors and are healed of a number of ailments. Most of us who know the Lord have benefited from medical treatment, as well. We have to use the practical sense God has given us.

Yet I always put my trust in God when I have a physical need. I really believe that God is the main healer. *"I am the* Lord *who heals you"* (Exodus 15:26). For example, I went to a Christian physician, and he discovered that I had a heart blockage. We prayed, and God healed me of this blockage. Other people with bad hearts have been healed in my meetings since this happened.

2. *Are people healed in only a certain way?*

One thing I have learned through my ministry travels and seeing God work in people's lives is never to second-guess God. Just when you think you have Him figured out or that He no longer performs the miraculous, He shows forth a great work.

We must be open to the various ways in which God may work. He loves us, and He wants us to know the depth of His concern for our well-being. Sometimes, we become so complacent in our conditions that we cease to call on the name of the Lord to help us.

Years ago, while I was in prayer, I had a vision of the Lord's banquet table. At the end of the table sat an outline of the Lord. There were hundreds of places set at the table, but only two seats were occupied. All the other seats were empty. The Lord asked me, "Where are the rest of them?"

"What, Lord?" I asked.

"Come and dine at the Master's table," was His only reply.

Then He began reminding me of a previous vision that He had shown me. In the middle of the night, I had dreamed of my kitchen—but it was a very elegant and spectacular version of the kitchen. In the natural, I had none of the things that filled this kitchen. But the kitchen had a set table that was fit for a king.

I had this dream night after night. And the Lord would say, "Come and dine at the Master's table. Come and dine." As I sat at the table, I kept noticing the empty chairs. Within what seemed like a two-hour period, only about ten people had joined the Lord at His table. As they came to the table, the Lord would speak to them and give them direction. The main point that I remember the Lord conveying was that we are to carry out the individual instructions that He has given to each of us. In other words, we have to throw off traditional ways of doing things. Any tradition that keeps us from seeking God with our whole hearts and entering into His presence is a hindrance. The religious leaders who rebuked Jesus for healing on the Sabbath were hindered by their self-imposed traditions. (See, for example, Luke 13:10–16.) We should not limit ourselves when it comes to seeking God and receiving from Him. Again, He may come when we least expect it

We should not limit ourselves when it comes to seeking God and receiving from Him.

and in a way that we hadn't thought He would show up in our lives.

In addition, at this table, God admonished all of us to walk in the shoes that He'd placed on our feet and not try to copy someone else's anointing. For instance, one person might have faith that God will heal him through the laying on of hands, while another might believe that God will heal her through the "miracle" of modern medicine. Whatever you do in life, do it in proportion to your faith. (See Romans 12:6–8.) In addition, don't put limits on God as He leads you. *"If you have faith as a mustard seed, you will say to this mountain, 'Move from here to there,' and it will move; and nothing will be impossible for you"* (Matthew 17:20).

God can heal in many different ways. When He healed the blind man, for instance, Jesus spat on the ground and used clay to anoint the man's eyes. (See John 9:1–7.) Can you imagine someone today spitting on the ground and then using the dirt to anoint your eyes? Your first instinct might be to back away. However, we must realize that God sometimes heals in an unusual way in order to shock the normal thinking of humankind and to focus their attention on Him as Healer. Healing, then, sometimes causes quite a commotion.

> He [Jesus] *said to him* [the blind man], *"Go, wash in the pool of Siloam"* (which is translated, Sent). *So he went and washed, and came back seeing. Therefore the neighbors and those who previously had seen that he was blind said, "Is not this he who sat and begged?" Some said, "This is he." Others said, "He is like him." He said, "I am he."* (John 9:7–9)

I believe that when the formerly blind man said, "*I am he*" (verse 9), it was because he wanted to leave nothing to speculation. He was making it clear that he once had been blind but now was able to see by the miraculous workings of God.

Again, throughout my travels, I often see God healing people through means that do not always coincide with our earthly ways of thinking. Sometimes, I actually see angels standing beside the pastor of a church as he or she prays for somebody. I can see the Word of God coming out of the pastor's mouth like a sword. As the person who is being prayed for is anointed with oil, the sword goes into that person and cuts out that dark spot from the sick individual's body.

Some people may feel heat on their bodies when they're being healed because God is touching them. They actually feel the witness and the warmth of the power of God. That is also why it is so important for us to believe God. Can you imagine how many more could have been healed at the same time the blind man was healed if they had only believed? Instead, the Pharisees and others wasted time doubting Jesus and calling Him a sinner when they should have been believing Him for a miracle!

People often ask me how to get the healing anointing of God. It's no big secret! Remain persistent in prayer and continue to seek the face of God. For hours, I have sought God, kneeled before His presence, and allowed Him to speak to me through dreams and visions. There are many things we could do for the Lord if we'd just take the time to seek Him and listen to what He has to say. For instance, there have been times when I have visited convalescent homes where some of the elderly patients were so ill that they had slipped into comas. Whether it was time for them to be healed or to go home to be with the Lord, I still prayed for them as if they could hear, because I knew that their spirits could hear my prayers.

I went to one rest home where the same preachers had been going for about ten years. I asked these preachers, "Why don't you lead these elderly people to the Lord?"

They answered, "They can't hear you."

"We must believe God and pray for them," I replied.

As we prayed for them, tears began to stream down the faces of those elderly people who were in a comatose state, and we led them to the Lord. Don't ever put limitations on God. *"For now we see in a mirror, dimly"* (1 Corinthians 13:12), but the more we come to know God, our understanding becomes enlightened. Unfortunately, because our conventional ways of thinking do not line up with God's supernatural manifestation, we unknowingly bind the Hand that holds the power to heal. Just remember, if God could raise Lazarus from the dead, surely He can heal us from sicknesses and diseases. Healing is a commission by God. He confirmed this fact when He sent the disciples out to preach with a purpose: *"And as you go, preach, saying, 'The kingdom of heaven is at hand.' Heal the sick, cleanse the lepers, raise the dead, cast out demons. Freely you have received, freely give"* (Matthew 10:7–8).

A misconception regarding healing is that God always saves people first and then heals them, but He also heals people to demonstrate His power in order to save them and others. The miraculous works of God speak for themselves, which is why Jesus said, *"Believe Me for the sake of the works themselves"* (John 14:11).

How many times might you have been in the presence of God when He was ready to heal and not known it? How many times have you traded the opportunity to receive a miracle for the hindrances that continue to stand between you and God? If you actually knew the answer to these questions, you might be dismayed.

God visits us often, but we fail to acknowledge His presence because we have been taught that He can show up only in a certain way or at a certain place. What if a beggar sat down beside you and said, "God sent me to lay hands on you to heal you"? Would you become turned off by this person's outward appearance and back away, or would you be able to sense the presence of God and receive the miracle God sent you that day? These are all very difficult questions, but ones that must be answered if we intend to ready ourselves for God's work in our lives. Whatever ails you is of great importance to God. He said in John 10:10 that He came that we might have life *more abundantly.* God wants to exceed your expectations and pour out a blessing that you will not have room to receive. (See Malachi 3:10.) He wants to heal you, bless you, and enable you to go out and lay hands on others and see them recover from their sicknesses. (See Mark 16:18.)

God wants to exceed your expectations and pour out a blessing that you will not have room to receive.

3. *What is the reason some people are not healed?*

The question many ask is, "Why do some people who have faith in God for healing remain sick or even die instead of being healed, as others are who seem to have the same faith?"

We don't know. There are many mysteries that we do not understand. We're not God, and we don't have all the answers. Ultimately, God has control over our destinies when it comes to living or dying.

Rather than focus on what might not be happening in regard to healing, it is better to emphasize the power and authority that God has made available to us to receive healing. In the Word of God, we see that some people tried to interpret God's thinking. They wasted time blaming people's illnesses on sin, or on their parents' sins, rather seeking a God-given cure for them.

In John 9, Jesus' disciples asked Him about the blind man, *"'Rabbi, who sinned, this man or his parents, that he was born blind?' Jesus answered, 'Neither this man nor his parents sinned, but that the works of God should be revealed in him'"* (verses 2–3). Jesus went on to explain that His job was to work the works of the One who sent Him. (See verse 4.) We might interpret this statement to mean that Jesus did not want to become bogged down with triviality. He had more important things to do, which were to heal the sick, raise the dead, and be the sacrifice for the sins of the world.

Whether we bring illness upon ourselves through bad eating habits, or whether illness just attacks us inexplicably, when we are sick, the only thing we want to know is, *How can I become healed from this ailment?* People who are sick or dying don't want to discuss whether they are sick because their parents have sinned. Instead, they seek God's mercy and relief. By equipping ourselves with the proper biblical knowledge concerning healing, we become better able to assist not only ourselves but also others who are in need.

None of us knows our appointed time to go home to be with the Lord. *"To everything there is a season, a time for every purpose under heaven: a time to be born, and a time to die....A time to kill, and a time to heal"* (Ecclesiastes 3:1–3). Although we have seen that there are times when God raises people from the dead, there are other times when, no matter how hard we pray, the person we pray for is not raised up in this life.

This does not mean, however, that we should not pray for complete healing. God encourages us to pray and to seek His face, not only to understand His will, but also to receive the desires of our hearts: *"Delight yourself also in the LORD, and He shall give you the desires of your heart"* (Psalm 37:4).

Likewise, sometimes God heals instantly, and sometimes He heals through a process. I had a heart blockage for two years before it was healed. I don't have all the answers, and I really don't know why God didn't heal it in the beginning. I think that is God's business. We know that by His stripes, we are healed. We see miracles, such as those shared in this book. So, I have truly learned to trust the Lord with everything. I've learned to lean on Him. I believe He's right on time.

4. *Do people's sins cause their sicknesses?*

Jesus said to the invalid whom He healed at the pool of Bethesda, *"See, you have been made well. Sin no more, lest a worse thing come upon you"* (John 5:14). There are times when sin will cause sickness or other forms of trouble in life. Sickness and death in general are a result of sin. (See Romans 5:12–14.) In the Old Testament, God sometimes used sickness to punish the Israelites for their disobedience and to draw them back to Him. (See Numbers 21:5– 9.) However, we must be careful not to pronounce that a certain illness was caused by specific sins. We must also realize that those who are sick do not always remain that way due to sin. One of the greatest misconceptions concerning healing is that those in need of a miracle might somehow have brought illness upon themselves. Again, as indicated in John 9, this is not always the case:

> *Now as Jesus passed by, He saw a man who was blind from birth. And His disciples asked Him, saying, "Rabbi, who sinned, this man or his parents, that he was born blind?" Jesus answered, "Neither this man nor his parents sinned, but that the works of God should be revealed in him."* (John 9:1–3)

The disciples were focusing on sin when, instead, they should have been focusing on the opportunity for onlookers to witness the miraculous power of God.

A related question that is often asked is, *Why do bad things happen to good people?* The Word of the Lord declares that in this life, we will all go through trials and tribulations, but that God is faithful to deliver us from them all. *"In the world you will have tribulation; but be of good cheer, I have overcome the world"* (John 16:33). Since Jesus has overcome and resides in us, then we, too, have the power to overcome "the world," including sickness and disease.

We will all go through trials and tribulations, but God is faithful to deliver us from them all.

Chapter 7

SCRIPTURAL PRESCRIPTIONS FOR HEALING

"Always pursue what is good both for yourselves and for all. Rejoice always, pray without ceasing, in everything give thanks; for this is the will of God in Christ Jesus for you. Do not quench the Spirit."
—1 Thessalonians 5:15–19

Earlier, we discussed the importance of accurately diagnosing the nature of the problems in our lives that need healing so that we can address them. After honestly evaluating our symptoms, we must consider important scriptural prescriptions for our healing. We have seen that God desires healing for all aspects of our lives: spirits, souls, and bodies. In this chapter, we will look at some foundational helps for healing—important ways in which we can cooperate with God as we seek wholeness.

Pray Individually and Corporately

The first scriptural prescription for healing is prayer. The word *prayer* has been used so often and so casually by many Christians that they tend to minimize the reality of this powerful connection to God.

The first step in prayer is to be clear about to whom we are praying. David prayed,

> *Give ear, O Lord, to my prayer; and attend to the voice of my supplications. In the day of my trouble I will call upon You, for You will answer me. Among the gods there is none like You, O Lord; nor are there any works like Your works. All nations whom You have made shall come and worship before You, O Lord, and shall glorify Your name. For You are great, and do wondrous things; You alone are God.*
> (Psalm 86:6–10)

If you will earnestly pray and seek God's face, you will begin to sense the power of His presence in your life.

A number of different religions and spiritual experiences are promoted in the world, especially through the secular media, and many people are confused and look to various "gods" to find help for their problems. They don't know the true and living God, or that real *"help comes from the Lord, the Maker of heaven and earth"* (Psalm 121:2 NIV). Two of the names of the Lord are *Jehovah Rapha,* our Healer (see Exodus 15:26), and *Jehovah Jireh,* our Provider (see Genesis 22:8–14). God wants to provide healing in the name of His Son Jesus. If you will earnestly pray and seek His face, you will begin to sense the power of His presence in your life.

The second step is to understand that prayer is not complicated; it is simply speaking to God with a sincere heart and making requests based on His Word and in the name of His Son Jesus. Don't be afraid to specifically articulate what you need to God.

Be anxious for nothing, but in everything by prayer and supplication, with thanksgiving, let your requests be made known to God; and the peace of God, which surpasses all understanding, will guard your hearts and minds through Christ Jesus. (Philippians 4:6–7)

Often, people are afraid to be specific with God for fear that they are asking for too much. Many times, they do not receive because they do not ask. James wrote, "*You do not have because you do not ask. You ask and do not receive, because you ask amiss, that you may spend it on your pleasures*" (James 4:2–3).

In addition, Jesus taught that we are to pray to the Father in His name:

You did not choose Me, but I chose you and appointed you that you should go and bear fruit, and that your fruit should remain, that whatever you ask the Father in My name He may give you. (John 15:16)

Most assuredly, I say to you, whatever you ask the Father in My name He will give you. Until now you have asked nothing in My name. Ask, and you will receive, that your joy may be full. (John 16:23–24)

Pray to God in the name of Jesus, who secured your salvation and healing through the stripes that He bore, through His death on the cross, and through His resurrection.

Third, we must see prayer as a form of worship, for when we ask God to heal us, we are ultimately saying to Him, "Only You, God, can give me what I need!" The Father loves it when we come to Him in sincere prayer with faith in our hearts. Jesus said, "*The hour is coming, and now is, when the true worshipers will worship the Father in spirit and truth; for the Father is seeking such to worship Him*" (John 4:23).

Fourth, we have to make prayer a priority in our lives and not something we do merely in our spare time. "*Now in the morning, having risen a long while before daylight, He [Jesus] went out and departed to a solitary place; and there He prayed*" (Mark 1:35). Whether you spend time in dedicated prayer early in the morning or at another time, let it be a natural and necessary part of your life.

Last, we need to recognize the power of corporate prayer in bringing healing.

> *And being let go, they [Peter and John] went to their own companions and reported all that the chief priests and elders had said to them. So when they heard that, they raised their voice to God with one accord and said:…"Lord, look on their threats, and grant to Your servants that with all boldness they may speak Your word, by stretching out Your hand to heal, and that signs and wonders may be done through the name of Your holy Servant Jesus." And when they had prayed, the place where they were assembled together was shaken; and they were all filled with the Holy Spirit, and they spoke the word of God with boldness.*
>
> (Acts 4:23–24, 29–31)

These early Christians prayed in power and unity, and God sent His Spirit among them, which resulted in miracles and healings:

> *And through the hands of the apostles many signs and wonders were done among the people. And they were*

all with one accord in Solomon's Porch....And believers were increasingly added to the Lord, multitudes of both men and women, so that they brought the sick out into the streets and laid them on beds and couches, that at least the shadow of Peter passing by might fall on some of them. Also a multitude gathered from the surrounding cities to Jerusalem, bringing sick people and those who were tormented by unclean spirits, and they were all healed. (Acts 5:12, 14–16)

These were the results of corporate prayer. Such prayer is vital, and it has become very important to me. Jesus said, *"If two of you agree on earth concerning anything that they ask, it will be done for them by My Father in heaven. For where two or three are gathered together in My name, I am there in the midst of them"* (Matthew 18:19–20). When I'm in a church and I know that the pastor and others there are hungry to see people set free, I always ask them to come up and join me in corporate prayer, and great results happen.

We read in the book of James,

Is anyone among you sick? Let him call for the elders of the church, and let them pray over him, anointing him with oil in the name of the Lord. And the prayer of faith will save the sick, and the Lord will raise him up. And if he has committed sins, he will be forgiven. Confess your trespasses to one another, and pray for one another, that you may be healed. (James 5:14–16)

In my meetings, I've had the elders come and join me in anointing people, and they've been healed. There was a precious man who was the pastor of a church. He was always shouting and praising the Lord. Then he got cancer. He went blind and ended up in the hospital. Some other ministers and I went to visit him to pray, and all I could do was cry and pray. I couldn't even say anything in English. I kept thinking, *Lord, I'd love for him to get back up and dance and praise You.* The doctors ordered X-rays taken, and they said they would have to take his bladder out. I was under heavy anointing, and I laid my hand on his stomach, along with the rest of the pastors, and we prayed and prayed and prayed. I went home and wept all evening in intercessory prayer for this man.

The next day, I received a phone call from the church, and they said, "Mary, it's a shock. They did an X-ray right before they were going to take his bladder out, and it's totally healed; there's no more cancer." In three weeks, this pastor was back in the church. He could see again, and he was dancing and praising the Lord. That was one of the greatest moves of God I have seen. I said, "Thank You, Jesus." It took corporate prayer as well as individual prayer. Sometimes, it takes corporate prayer to break strongholds off people. The other factor was that this man wanted deliverance, and he exercised his faith for healing.

Read, Study, and Apply God's Word

A second prescription for healing is the Word of God. *"Study to show thyself approved unto God, a workman that needeth not to be ashamed, rightly dividing the word of truth"* (2 Timothy 2:15 KJV). The more you study the Word of God, the less likely you will be deterred from your healing by unbiblical teachings, false doctrines, the devil's deceptions, and emotional discouragement. *"My son, give* attention to my words; incline your ear to my sayings. Do not let them depart from your eyes; keep them in the midst of your heart; for they are life to those who find them, and health to all their flesh" (Proverbs 4:20–22).

Furthermore, the more you allow the Word of God to permeate your spirit, the stronger you will become spiritually and the more determined you will be to persevere. The Word of God is life and good health, and the

> *The Word of God is life and good health.*

more we read it, the more God's infinite possibilities resonate in our lives. Every day, whether you feel like or not, set aside time to read, study, and understand the Scriptures. Fill your mind with God's Word and meditate on it. Have faith in His Word—believing, speaking, and acting on it. Fight for your healing and do not give up. *"Then they cried out to the LORD in their trouble, and He saved them out of their distresses. He sent His word and healed them, and delivered them from their destructions"* (Psalm 107:19–20).

Upon hearing bad news regarding their health, many people mistakenly begin speaking death. The Scriptures say, *"A man's stomach shall be satisfied from the fruit of his mouth, from the produce of his lips he shall be filled. Death and life are in the power of the tongue"* (Proverbs 18:20–21). Words are the sustenance of your well-being. You are either nourished by what you speak or contaminated by it.

In Matthew 8, we read about the centurion who put total his trust in Jesus and the authority of His words:

> *Now when Jesus had entered Capernaum, a centurion came to Him, pleading with Him, saying, "Lord, my servant is lying at home paralyzed, dreadfully*

tormented." And Jesus said to him, "I will come and heal him." The centurion answered and said, "Lord, I am not worthy that You should come under my roof. But only speak a word, and my servant will be healed. For I also am a man under authority, having soldiers under me. And I say to this one, 'Go,' and he goes; and to another, 'Come,' and he comes; and to my servant, 'Do this,' and he does it." When Jesus heard it, He marveled, and said to those who followed, "Assuredly, I say to you, I have not found such great faith, not even in Israel! And I say to you that many will come from east and west, and sit down with Abraham, Isaac, and Jacob in the kingdom of heaven. But the sons of the kingdom will be cast out into outer darkness. There will be weeping and gnashing of teeth." Then Jesus said to the centurion, "Go your way; and as you have believed, so let it be done for you." And his servant was healed that same hour.   (Matthew 8:5–13)

God wants to break those yokes off you!

Perhaps you are currently going through things that you haven't told anybody about. God wants to break those yokes off you! There are sicknesses that God wants to deliver you from if you will just yield to His voice and submit your will to His will.

You also have to fight the devil with the Word of God. Again, God didn't say that we wouldn't go through things in life, but He did say that we hold the power to overcome them. "*No weapon formed against you shall prosper*" (Isaiah 54:17). You have to hit the devil with the Word of God. You are already buried and risen in Christ Jesus (see Ephesians

2:4–6), so command the enemy to go back to the pits of hell from where he came. You have to show the devil that you mean business, and the only way to do that is through the power of the Word of God and the Spirit of God.

Guard Your Heart and Mind

As you seek healing, a third prescription is to guard your heart and mind. It is important to separate yourself from those who continually have a negative outlook on life and who don't believe God's Word. When you need healing, you must block out all unconstructive influences, build up your faith, and seek God with your whole heart. Keep your mind focused on the Healer. *"You will keep him in perfect peace, whose mind is stayed on You, because he trusts in You. Trust in the LORD forever, for in YAH, the LORD, is everlasting strength"* (Isaiah 26:3–4). If you can think of at least one positive thing to hold on to as you are waiting for the manifestation of your healing to come forth, it is worth holding on to.

Perhaps you are thinking, *I've tried all of this and none of it is working.* Again, don't give up. God does not give up on you, and neither should you give up when it comes to believing Him for your healing. Today, more than ever, those who belong to the body of Christ must draw strength from God and depend upon Him to meet their needs.

As I wrote earlier, many people in the world are desperately searching for the true and living God, yet television, the Internet, movies, radio, and magazines are permeated with all types of false doctrines. Many times, it is our testimonies that will give others the strength to persevere as they see the true God living in us and working through us.

Moreover, when you are in need of healing, it can be a very lonely experience. Those around you may not know what to say to bring comfort, or they may fear saying the wrong thing and not say anything at all. As much as we like to confide in those whom we love, often they are unable to give us the relief that we so desperately need. Sometimes, you can feel as if you are screaming out loud, yet no one seems to hear. Life appears to move in slow motion around you as others go about their usual activities; it can seem as if you are the only one on earth going through something difficult. Yet you don't always know what other people are going through. Likewise, others may not realize what you are experiencing.

During those times, keep focused on God, His Word, and His unfailing love. *"The eyes of the LORD are on those who fear [reverence] him, on those whose hope is in his unfailing love"* (Psalm 33:18 NIV). Remember that as you pray and give God your concerns, *"the peace of God, which surpasses all understanding, will guard your hearts and minds through Christ Jesus"* (Philippians 4:7).

We all have this in common: God is the answer to our needs. He wants us to know that He has not forgotten us, and neither is He ignoring our cries for help. When we feel empty, God fills us with *"newness of life"* (Romans 6:4).

This is what the Sovereign LORD, the Holy One of Israel, says: "In repentance and rest is your salvation, in quietness and trust is your strength...." Yet the LORD longs to be gracious to you; he rises to show you compassion. For the LORD is a God of justice. Blessed are all who wait for him! O people of Zion, who live in Jerusalem, you will weep no more. How

gracious he will be when you cry for help!
(Isaiah 30:15, 18–19 NIV)

Incorporate Songs of Praise

In keeping with guarding our hearts and minds, songs of praise are another important prescription for healing. A friend and I went to Brazil to minister some years ago. Our hosts picked us up one night to take us to pray for a lady who had brain damage due to head trauma. She was only twenty-five years old and had small children. This woman had been lying on her back for six weeks, and the doctors said that she was going to die.

When we arrived at her house, she was in so much pain that she couldn't lift her head. We went in to pray, and the Holy Spirit prompted us to sing, "I Am the Lord that Healeth Thee." Together, my friend and I saw a vision of what looked like a beam of light coming down into that woman's head in the exact spot where the trauma had occurred. I told our interpreter to tell the people what we saw. They began to shout and cry, and the injured woman began to pray in tongues. A few days after we left, we received news that two days after we had prayed, the woman had gotten up and begun caring for herself. She was totally healed. He is truly *"the Lord who heals you"* (Exodus 15:26).

Bishop Bloomer gives this account of the impact of songs on healing a man who was near death:

"One Tuesday night, during our weekly Sit and Share Bible Study, I was ministering on the topics of dominion and the authority of every believer. There was an unusual anointing that night. It felt like a crusade, a camp meeting, or an old-fashioned revival meeting. What was supposed to have been a night of teaching turned into an anointed night of preaching.

"All of a sudden, it seemed as if the entire sanctuary was filled with smoke. It was a fog, a light mist, and I wondered if I was the only one who was seeing it. I would periodically blink my eyes several times to see if the mist had anything to do with me. After all, I had been preaching hard and had worshiped heavily and was crying. No matter how many times I blinked, however, the mist remained, as if it wanted me to acknowledge it. I believe it was the glory of God.

"As the worshipers were quieting, a woman shouted, 'I'm healed. Jesus healed me!'"

"As we were concluding the worship portion of the meeting, the room was filled with praises: 'Thank You, Jesus…hallelujah…glory to God!' Some people were speaking in their heavenly languages (see 1 Corinthians 13:1), and it was glorious! Some were 'slain' in the Spirit (falling down under the Spirit's influence), many were crying, and all were praising God. It seemed like the day of Pentecost, with the Holy Spirit making His presence known. The minister of music was playing the song 'How Great Is Our God,' and as the worshipers were quieting, a woman shouted out, 'He's here… He's here…I can feel Him…He's here!' and then shouted, 'I'm healed. Jesus healed me! Look! There, right there, do you see it?' She was referring to same mist in the air that I had seen. My question was answered. She, too, had seen the cloud of glory indicating the presence of God. What I had been hesitant to acknowledge publicly, she acknowledged with confidence and faith.

"When she finished speaking, another woman ran to the altar, weeping, and said, 'God told me to come here tonight to see you, the man of God, and I am so glad I did. My husband is in a coma; a drunk driver came over the barrier from the left side into the right lane and hit him head-on. He broke his arms, his legs, and his neck. It's a wonder he is still breathing, and he has not opened his eyes in four months. Some have said he is dead; the machine is breathing for him. But God told me to come see you. I am so glad I obeyed Him. Bishop, I have never felt the anointing and the presence of God like this. God is here in this place. I believe that if you pray for my husband, God will raise him up from his deathbed.'

"So, I prayed, and while I was praying, the Lord spoke to my heart, *Song. Give her a song!* Then He said, *Sing. She needs songs.* I turned to her and asked, 'Where is your husband now?' She answered, 'At Wake Medical.' I said, 'Immediately after the service, I will go with you to lay hands on him and believe that God will raise him up.' When I spoke that word, she began to weep, jump, and rejoice. The Lord spoke to me yet again and said, *Songs.* I had no idea what God was talking about, so I started thinking of a song I could sing to this woman's husband at the hospital.

"When I arrived at his hospital room, I was shocked and horrified at his appearance. He had not spoken in four months. He was hooked to a machine that looked as if it was breathing for him, and he was in a full body cast, with parts of his body elevated. Doubt hit me as I questioned under my breath, *What are you doing here, and what have you gotten yourself into?* I put on my best 'poker face' and prayed a fervent prayer.

"Then, God spoke, *Songs!* So, I instructed everyone to hold hands, and I began to sing, 'Surely goodness and mercy shall follow me all the days of my life.' We sang it powerfully, but I was empty. God had said *Songs*, and I felt that this wasn't the song that He was talking about.

"Then I remembered that I had just recorded thirteen songs on a CD entitled *Songs of Jabez* and that I had one of the CDs in my car. I gave it to his wife and instructed her to play it every day, nonstop. She followed my instruction. On day one, after six hours of listening to the CD, this man opened his eyes. On day two, he started breathing on his own. On day three, he developed a way to communicate by blinking his eyes: once for yes, twice for no. On days four and five, he started forming words. And the music continued to play. Two weeks later, he was talking, feeling sensations in his arms, legs, and back, and eating solid foods.

God healed a man in a coma through songs based on His Word.

"God healed him! Not through the faithless prayer of a preacher who was discouraged by what he saw, but by songs based on God's Word. That was seven years ago, and the man is now back at work. He is driving, bicycling, and playing tennis. Oh, what a testimony he has! There was healing in the songs. Humanity usually looks at conditions, but the healing power of God's Word in those songs accomplished what the Word was sent to do, and that was to minister to the man's spirit and not to his intellect. God says, '*My word that goes out from my mouth…will not return to me empty, but will accomplish what I desire and achieve the purpose for which I sent it*' (Isaiah 55:11 NIV).

"Sometimes, when you run out of words, God will give you a song—a song of deliverance to bring healing to your ailing soul. David wrote, *'You are my hiding place; You shall preserve me from trouble; You shall surround me with songs of deliverance'* (Psalm 32:7). When Saul was wrathful against David, David played anointed music, and I believe this music allowed him to escape death by Saul's spear. (See 1 Samuel 18:10–11.) God will use whatever means necessary to deliver you from the hand of the enemy, for His anointing knows no bounds."

"Psalm 22:3 says, *'Thou art holy, O thou that inhabitest the praises of Israel'* (kjv). The Lord inhabits the praises of His people. He honors heartfelt songs of praise with His presence, and He frequently brings blessing and healing in response to them."

Seek Forgiveness and Purity of Heart

Two additional and significant prescriptions for healing are forgiveness and purity of heart. We cannot afford to hold bitterness and hatred in our hearts because doing so prevents us from approaching God and receiving from Him what we need. For example, the Scriptures say,

For if you forgive men their trespasses, your heavenly Father will also forgive you. But if you do not forgive men their trespasses, neither will your Father forgive your trespasses. (Matthew 6:14–15)

Husbands, likewise, dwell with them with understanding, giving honor to the wife, as to the weaker vessel, and as being heirs together of the grace of life, that your prayers may not be hindered. (1 Peter 3:7)

Right relationships are important for having our prayers answered. I always stress repentance and being forthright with God. Toxic attitudes in us do nothing but fuel the devil's flame against us. Once, in a vision, I saw thousands of rooms in heaven filled with books. Each of us has a book in heaven with our record in it. It records every single thing that we do throughout each day. Think about that the next time you consider holding a grudge against someone. In another vision, I saw one man begin confessing his sins before God: "I'm a sinner, I'm a liar, I'm a drunk," and so forth. With each sin that he confessed, what looked like big black bands began dropping from his wrists. He began to praise and worship God because the Lord was setting him free, and he was being healed by the power of God.

Bitterness is the host for all sorts of sicknesses that can be healed only by applying the antidote of forgiveness. Forgiveness is one of the greatest medications on earth. It releases anger and resentment and mends the brokenhearted.

We must also desire and seek purity of heart in all aspects of our lives. We receive the righteousness of God through Christ when we are saved. (See 2 Corinthians 5:21.) Yet, throughout our lives, we need to continually yield ourselves to God, choose His will over the desires of the fleshly nature, and dedicate ourselves to Him:

> How can a young man cleanse his way? By taking heed according to Your word. With my whole heart I have sought You; oh, let me not wander from Your commandments! (Psalm 119:9–10)

> In a large house there are articles not only of gold and silver, but also of wood and clay; some are for noble

purposes and some for ignoble. If a man cleanses himself from the latter, he will be an instrument for noble purposes, made holy, useful to the Master and prepared to do any good work. Flee the evil desires of youth, and pursue righteousness, faith, love and peace, along with those who call on the Lord out of a pure heart.   (2 Timothy 2:20–22 NIV)

The devil comes to steal, kill, and destroy, but Jesus comes to give you life more abundantly. (See John 10:10.) At the name of Jesus, demons run. As we forgive others and pursue holiness, knowing that our righteousness comes from Christ, we can approach God and receive the healing we need.

Therefore, brethren, having boldness to enter the Holiest by the blood of Jesus, by a new and living way which He consecrated for us, through the veil, that is, His flesh, and having a High Priest over the house of God, let us draw near with a true heart in full assurance of faith, having our hearts sprinkled from an evil conscience and our bodies washed with pure water. Let us hold fast the confession of our hope without wavering, for He who promised is faithful. And let us consider one another in order to stir up love and good works, not forsaking the assembling of ourselves together, as is the manner of some, but exhorting one another, and so much the more as you see the Day approaching. (Hebrews 10:19–25)

Release the Power of Faith and Testimony

A final prescription for healing is the power of testimony. Many years ago, I was being trained in ministry by a wonderful mentor who was under the tutelage of A. A. Allen. At one of the services we attended, a young man came who had suffered brain damage. As a result, he dragged one of his legs when he walked. My mentor was preaching when the man sat down beside me in the front row and whispered to me, "I came for a miracle." When he said this, the Lord immediately said to me, *That man is going to get healed tonight.*

After my mentor finished her message, she called me up and explained that the two of us, along with the ministers, were going to pray for the congregation. That young man came up and gave his life to the Lord. Then, I went over to him and asked, "Son, what happened to you?" He explained, "I was coming home late one night from a bar when five men jumped me and beat me up with a baseball bat and I almost died. I remained in the hospital for weeks. But when my neighbor invited me to church tonight and told me that I would get a miracle, I felt joy leap inside of me."

So we anointed him with oil and began to pray. There were about six of us praying for him, and I laid my hand on the area that was damaged. Because I have seen God give people new brain cells in the past, I recognized that this man was being set free. I saw an angel of the Lord begin working on this young man's brain. Then, I saw what looked like a bowl with a mixture of various colors circling around in it, and I knew that God was giving him new brain cells. Suddenly, this young man began to shout and run all over the church. He began praising God with everything in him because God had brought total restoration to him.

When that man's neighbor had told him of God's power to heal him, the Spirit of God had confirmed it to him, he had believed it, and he came and received his healing.

I used to go to Norway to preach, and the pastor there would look over at a group in wheelchairs and say, "Okay, by the end of the night, you're going to throw that wheelchair away and get up and walk, in Jesus' name!" And sure enough, by the end of the night, people would be walking around who had been bound for years by different ailments and afflictions.

Earlier, I mentioned how supernatural teeth fillings had occurred at meetings when people gave their testimonies about their teeth being filled by God. I have seen this happen in regard to other ailments, as well. In addition, when people witness someone miraculously healed by God, it becomes a testimony to believers and nonbelievers alike—a demonstration that nothing is impossible to those who believe. (See Mark 9:23.)

When people witness someone miraculously healed by God, it becomes a demonstration that nothing is impossible to those who believe.

As you seek healing, build your faith through the testimonies of others and the truth of the Word of God that they speak to you. And as you minister healing to others, testify about your own healing and other things that God has done in your life because it will serve to increase their faith.

The prescriptions for healing we have been looking at are prayer, God's Word, guarding your heart and mind, incorporating praise, seeking forgiveness and purity of heart, and releasing the power of faith and testimony. These foundations of life in Christ will keep you close to God, enable you to discern His voice, and build up your faith. Start living in the fullness of the Spirit today as you seek healing for your life.

Chapter 8

COUNTERACTING HINDRANCES TO HEALING

"With men it is impossible, but not with God; for with God all things are possible."
—Mark 10:27

A long with applying the prescriptions for healing, we must counteract various hindrances that may be blocking our healing from God. The account of Jesus' healing of the lame man at the pool of Bethesda will help us to identify some these hindrances:

> *After this there was a feast of the Jews, and Jesus went up to Jerusalem. Now there is in Jerusalem by the Sheep Gate a pool, which is called in Hebrew, Bethesda, having five porches. In these lay a great multitude of sick people, blind, lame, paralyzed, waiting for the moving of the water. For an angel went down at a certain time into the pool and stirred up the water; then whoever stepped in first, after the stirring of the water, was made well of whatever disease he had. Now a certain man was there who had an infirmity thirty-eight years.*

When Jesus saw him lying there, and knew that he already had been in that condition a long time, He said to him, "Do you want to be made well?" The sick man answered Him, "Sir, I have no man to put me into the pool when the water is stirred up; but while I am coming, another steps down before me." Jesus said to him, "Rise, take up your bed and walk." And immediately the man was made well, took up his bed, and walked. And that day was the Sabbath. The Jews therefore said to him who was cured, "It is the Sabbath; it is not lawful for you to carry your bed." He answered them, "He who made me well said to me, 'Take up your bed and walk.'" Then they asked him, "Who is the Man who said to you, 'Take up your bed and walk'?" But the one who was healed did not know who it was, for Jesus had withdrawn, a multitude being in that place. Afterward Jesus found him in the temple, and said to him, "See, you have been made well. Sin no more, lest a worse thing come upon you." (John 5:1–14)

There was a pool in Jerusalem called Bethesda that had five porches. The name *Bethesda* means "house of kindness." The porches of Bethesda were filled with a multitude of people who were sick with blindness, lameness, and paralysis. They were all awaiting one thing: *"the moving of the water"* (verse 3).

Notice that when Jesus came to the pool, He and the man with the *"infirmity"* were focused on two different things. Jesus was focused on His power to heal him: *"Do you want to be made well?"* (verse 6). The man, however, was focused on the hindrances that had kept him from being healed: *"Sir, I have no man to put me into the pool when the water is stirred up; but while I am coming, another steps down before me"* (verse 7).

Excuses can be major hindrances preventing us from receiving our miracles from God. Spiritual, mental, and even physical effort may be involved in our deliverances, especially when we have developed many excuses to remain in our predicaments. For example, you may not be fully delivered simply by rising from your sickbed. You may need to make major changes in your lifestyle. That is why Jesus asked the question, *"Do you want to be made well?"* When Jesus heals, He does not heal just a leg, a foot, or eyes. He touches every area of our lives that needs deliverance. He told the man not only to rise but also to take up his bed and walk, and He warned him that he needed to stop sinning and turn to God.

Jesus touches every area of our lives that needs deliverance.

When you not only rise but also "pick up your bed" and walk in God's ways, you are really healed. This truth applies to every area of your life that needs healing—your body, mind, emotions, finances, family relationships, sexuality, work habits, responsibility, and so forth. We can apply Paul's words to the Galatians in this regard: *"Stand fast therefore in the liberty by which Christ has made us free, and do not be entangled again with a yoke of bondage"* (Galatians 5:1).

Let us look now at particular pitfalls that can hinder us in our healing.

A Mind-set of Defeat

Again, when Jesus asked the man who had the infirmity for thirty-eight years, *"Do you want to be made well?"*

(John 5:6), he replied, *"Sir, I have no man to put me into the pool when the water is stirred up; but while I am coming, another steps down before me"* (verse 7). He never really answered Jesus' question.

According to the man, he constantly missed his miracle because he had no one to place him in the water once it was stirred by the angel. Therefore, he continued to suffer while others around him were healed. This man had dealt with his ailment for almost four decades, yet no one had found it in his or her heart to assist this man as he sought his healing. Apparently, friends or family members did at least drop him off at the pool, but why did they not remain to put him *into* the pool when the waters moved? It is possible that it was because he'd made a mistake that many of us make today. Perhaps he had surrounded himself with people who were merely tolerating him instead of those who actually cared for him. Many times, we allow our environments to keep us in the same predicament. Those with whom you connect can have a significant impact on your receiving what you need from God. This man had all but given up on being able to be healed. He had a mind-set of defeat.

Do you want to be healed? If so, then don't become a complainer or dwell on negatives; just receive your healing! Jesus took no time to entertain the man's excuses. He simply told him to take up his bed and walk. When seeking your healing, it is vital to follow Jesus' instructions.

I went to pray for a woman who was in the hospital with a tumor. She was only thirty-five years old, and she had children, but she had already resigned herself to death and had written out her will. I told her, "Jesus can heal you." She said, "Oh, no, I've had my last rites; I don't want to live." I said, "Well, can I please pray for you?"

This woman was in a lot of pain. I prayed with her, and right before our eyes, the swelling in her stomach disappeared within five minutes. She was in total shock because of what God had done for her. But then she turned and said to me, "I've made my will out. I'm still going to die." I talked to her and prayed for her, and I counseled her about the love of God and the power of the cross. Then I left, and two days later, I got a phone call that she had died.

This outcome truly grieved my heart, and it makes it difficult to include this story in this book. She did not want to live. She did not want to believe the gospel of Jesus Christ. As an evangelist and a preacher, I meet all types of people who are sick. Some of them don't want to know Jesus. They think they might as well give up.

The man at Bethesda had an "*infirmity*" for decades. In addition to a sickness or disease, however, a person's "infirmity" can be an entrenched thought process. Many of us are infirm by our ways of thinking. We think *poor*, so we are poor; we think *loneliness*, so we're lonely; we think *unhappiness*, so we're unhappy. Philippians 2:5 urges us, "*Let this mind be in you which was also in Christ Jesus*," but we often do not let the mind of Christ—through the Holy Spirit and the Word of God—direct our lives. Why? We live in a society and a world consumed with priorities and values that are not God's, and we take these priorities and values for ourselves.

Let the mind of Christ— through the Holy Spirit and the Word of God—direct your life.

Life has much to do with the choices that we make, and our choices have much do with our upbringings. The way we treat ourselves and the way we treat those who come into our lives are often based upon beliefs that have been instilled within us through our families, through our life experiences as we have grown older, and through our cultures.

As a result, certain embedded mind-sets and attitudes can hinder our healings. Have you adopted a mind-set of defeat or complacency that is not open to what God can do for you? You don't know what plans God may have for you, so keep placing your trust and faith in Him.

Life can seem intimidating sometimes. We feel beaten up by life. However, do you want to know how to shock life? After life "runs you over," get up again. Make a conscious decision to live and not die because of the love and power of God.

A Mind-set of Unbelief

Jesus healed a man who had been born blind, but a number of the Pharisees refused to accept this miracle, as well as the fact that Jesus had come from God.

> *Jesus said, "For judgment I have come into this world, that those who do not see may see, and that those who see may be made blind." Then some of the Pharisees who were with Him heard these words, and said to Him, "Are we blind also?" Jesus said to them, "If you were blind, you would have no sin; but now you say, 'We see.' Therefore your sin remains."*
> (John 9:39–41)

Mark Twain once said, "It ain't what you don't know that gets you into trouble. It's what you know for sure that just ain't so." Remaining obstinate in your way of thinking, especially when your mind is filled with wrong information, will ultimately get you into trouble.

Jesus was very direct and penetrating in His assessment of these Pharisees' inability to receive salvation and healing for their own lives. He pointed out that because they claimed to have all the answers and continually rejected God's truth, they remained separated from God. If they had allowed themselves to receive the love of God into their lives instead of constantly rejecting it, they, too, could have experienced the joy of spiritual, mental, and emotional healing.

"*Love...does not rejoice in iniquity, but rejoices in the truth*" (1 Corinthians 13:4, 6). The truth is that God is a Healer who sent His Son, Jesus Christ, to be the Savior of the world. Sometimes, the way we see things can get in the way of our miracles. When people insist on seeing only with their natural eyes and continually refuse to acknowledge the power of God, even when it is demonstrated right in front of them, they cannot expect to receive healing from Him. If you discount Jesus' salvation, thinking you know better, "*your sin remains*" (John 9:41), and often, so does your illness.

Even in Jesus' own hometown of Nazareth, He could perform no miracles because His work was disregarded instead of embraced:

> *And when the Sabbath had come, He began to teach in the synagogue. And many hearing Him were astonished, saying, "Where did this Man get these things? And what wisdom is this which is given to Him, that such mighty works are performed by His hands! Is this not the carpenter, the Son of Mary, and brother of*

James, Joses, Judas, and Simon? And are not His sisters here with us?" So they were offended at Him. But Jesus said to them, "A prophet is not without honor except in his own country, among his own relatives, and in his own house." Now He could do no mighty work there, except that He laid His hands on a few sick people and healed them. And He marveled because of their unbelief. (Mark 6:2–6)

An Atmosphere of Fear or Depression

Another hindrance to healing that we must counteract is an atmosphere of fear and depression. The hearts of many people "[fail] *them from fear"* (Luke 21:26) when they hear bad news. Sicknesses can be provoked by demonic influences that come to kill, steal, and destroy our sense of well-being through fear. (See John 10:10.) And such influences can also prevent our healing if we accept what they say instead of what God's Word says.

For instance, upon hearing the news of a financial recession, many people immediately begin to feel ill. A "recession" has two components: lack of funding and depression. With the threat of a loss of income or the reality of it, some individuals want to retreat to their beds and pull the covers over their heads because recession has given birth to depression in them.

In 1933, during the Great Depression, about 25 percent of workers were unemployed. This meant that a large number of families either went without food or scarcely had enough to eat. Consequently, both physical and mental problems began taking a toll on the lives of heads of households who could no longer afford to support themselves or their families. Many began self-medicating on cheap wine. These people experienced a recession that depressed them, and they added to that depression a habit or addiction that oppressed them. They felt there was no one to help them—or they did not want to accept help from others—and there seemed to be no way out. They were living in physical, mental, and emotional states of depression. Such states of mind and heart extract strength from individuals by bringing to the surface their moral weaknesses.

The effects of economic and social uncertainties or their own personal troubles may cause people today to become afraid and depressed and to try to deal with their pain through various forms of destructive habits and practices. Yet those who know Christ do not have to respond to life's uncertainties with fear. We are not those *"having no hope and without God in the world"* (Ephesians 2:12). Instead, we are *"members of the household of God"* (verse 19). And Jesus promised that our heavenly Father would take care of us.

Those who know Christ do not have to respond to life's uncertainties with fear.

> Do not worry, saying, "What shall we eat?" or "What shall we drink?" or "What shall we wear?" For after all these things the Gentiles seek. For your heavenly Father knows that you need all these things. But seek first the kingdom of God and His righteousness, and all these things shall be added to you.
>
> (Matthew 6:31–33)

142 A Divine Revelation of Healing

Whether your fear has caused your illness, or your illness has created fear within you, remember that *"God has not given us a spirit of fear, but of power and of love and of a sound mind"* (2 Timothy 1:7). Do not allow the enemy to rob you of the peace that Christ has given you. Instead of looking to the circumstances, trust in God's strength and in the power of His Word.

A Habit of Isolating Ourselves

Being self-sufficient or individualistic is often celebrated in our society. We like to think that we don't need anyone else. Yet the Bible explicitly tells us,

> *And let us consider one another in order to stir up love and good works, not forsaking the assembling of ourselves together, as is the manner of some, but exhorting one another, and so much the more as you see the Day approaching.* (Hebrews 10:24–25)

We must counteract the attitude or habit of isolating ourselves from others, especially when we need healing. One of the devil's most cunning tricks is seclusion because he knows that where two or three are gathered together in Jesus' name, there you will find the Spirit of God in the midst of them. (See Matthew 18:20.) Once the Spirit of God comes in the name of Jesus where sickness dwells, sickness has to flee!

We need to surround ourselves with those who hold the power to call upon the name of the Lord and to receive what they need from God. For thirty-eight years, the invalid at the pool apparently had not developed a relationship with anyone willing to help him get into the water.

The Bible says, *"Cast your bread upon the waters, for you will find it after many days"* (Ecclesiastes 11:1). This means that your harvest is a result of your seed. Therefore, your seed has the potential to determine how you will eventually live. You can knowingly or unknowingly sow your present circumstances—whether good or bad—by having strong, supportive relationships or by being isolated from others.

Break free from an attitude of isolation and reach out for the spiritual and emotional support of other believers.

"A man who has friends must himself be friendly" (Proverbs 18:24). We must develop relationships with others who are spiritually minded and can support us when we need prayer. Have you ever been so desperate that you no longer cared what others thought? You just knew you needed a miracle, and you were willing to go to great extremes to receive it. Break free from an attitude of isolation and reach out for the spiritual and emotional support of other believers.

Sometimes, the isolation we experience is not one of our own making. People may leave us when we need them the most. Yet no matter who bails out of our lives when we experience trouble, God is always with us. The second part of Proverbs 18:24 reads, *"But there is a friend who sticks closer than a brother."* Who but God is our greatest Friend? John wrote in 1 John 1:3, *"That which we have seen and heard we declare to you, that you also may have fellowship with us; and truly our fellowship is with the Father and with His Son Jesus Christ."* Don't ever become so consumed by your condition that you isolate yourself from God and miss His presence in your time of need.

A Failure to Move On

Another hindrance to counteract is the temptation to put your full reliance on people or things rather than God. Again, many people can simply think themselves into trouble. In other words, the way they were raised to view the world or the bad teaching they adopted can become more influential than their commitment to God. Bishop Bloomer gives this sobering account of a woman who had this mind-set:

"A lady came to me some time ago asking for prayer because one of her legs was shorter than the other, and she was walking with a cane. I laid hands on her and began to pray. She fell out in the Spirit, and when she finally came to herself, she was healed: her leg had grown to a normal length. Following the service, she came to me and asked, 'Can I have my cane back?' I asked her why she needed the cane since it was obvious that God had healed her completely. Her answer upset me greatly.

"'Well, Bishop,' she began to explain, 'I get a check every month, and if I don't have my cane they might cut off my check.'

"I then made it clear to her, 'Look, there was an evil spirit on you, and if I give you this cane back, whatever was attached to you is coming back.'

"'I need my check,' was her response. And she took the cane.

"Today, this lady is in a wheelchair with both legs amputated. This is not to imply that recurring sickness is always due to disobedience, but simply to point out that when God is trying to bring you into your healing, you cannot allow the fear of losing other things around you to get in the way of your miracle."

Trust God completely! *"Ask in faith, with no doubting, for he who doubts is like a wave of the sea driven and tossed by the wind"* (James 1:6). When you allow yourself to be carried by the waves of doubt, you are trusting in the unreliable elements of your physical environment to care for you instead of relying on God. In addition to your physical healing, you must adopt the way of thinking that the man at Bethesda had after his miracle. After being interrogated by the religious authorities regarding why he was carrying his bed on the Sabbath, the man replied, *"He who made me well said to me, 'Take up your bed and walk'"* (John 5:11).

The man at Bethesda did not even know who Jesus was, but at His word, the man believed and was healed and set free. (See John 5:13.) When you call upon the name of God and hold on to His promises, your life will begin to change. Yet, for some people, the very thing that had brought them a degree of comfort keeps them bound because they want to keep depending on it.

When you call upon the name of God and hold on to His promises, your life will begin to change.

Once you are healed, you must lay aside any "crutches" that have sustained your illness and begin walking in newness of life, regardless of what those around you may think. *"Lay aside every weight, and the sin which so easily ensnares us, and let us run with endurance the race that is set before us, looking unto Jesus, the author and finisher of our faith"* (Hebrews 12:1–2).

Many people think that their illnesses or diseases are their problem in life. Instead, it is their attitude toward life that is the problem. They have stepped outside of life because they are determined to live in ways that are not in line with God and His purposes, and they have no intention of changing their ways. Their own desires and ideologies are stronger than their faith and commitment to God. They may ask for a little help from God, but then they decide to rely on something outside of Him. We all have weaknesses, but when we give in to them with no remorse or repentance, we cannot claim that the enemy tempted us. Our actions were the result of our own self-destructive and self-gratifying intentions.

Everyone else at the pool had apparently conditioned themselves to think that healing from God could take place only at that pool. But after thirty-eight years of suffering from the same illness, the invalid received a visit from Jesus because Jesus knew that he was ready to receive the revolutionary change that was about to take place in his life. Hundreds of people could have been healed that day, but perhaps their minds were not open enough to receive what Jesus had for them.

If you hang around people who are content with their conditions, you may begin to take on their deteriorative states, as well as become complacent with your own. That is why God commands in 2 Corinthians 6:17, *"Come out from among them and be separate."* The man was the only one at the porch who was able to receive a new concept and way of being healed besides being placed in the pool. Jesus did not have to touch the man; He did not perform a ceremony or even sprinkle him with oil. He simply said to Him, *"Rise, take up your bed and walk"* (John 5:8). He spoke a word of authority against the sick man's condition, and the man was made well.

After he was healed, the man left the porch because if he had remained there, his ailment would likely have returned. Perhaps you have been healed from a sickness, an ailment, or another type of infirmity, but after your healing, you returned to the source of your sickness. The woman whose leg was healed when Bishop Bloomer prayed for her held on to a crippling mind-set and ended up in worse bondage. Once God touches you and sets you free from something and you return to the source of your ailment, "the spirit returns seven times worse." (See Luke 11:24–26.)

There are a number of ways in which we can fail to move on after our healings. As we saw in chapter 2, part of our responsibility in healing is to take care of our bodies. Not living a balanced life by eating right, exercising, taking time for rest, and following the doctor's orders can sow bad health. Again, our predicaments can be related to the choices we make. People can abuse their own health. Many people become sick and afflicted through their own neglect or bad habits. There's a certain responsibility we need to take for our health.

There are people who think they can neglect their health or ignore wise medical advice and then just ask God to heal them. It is God's desire for them to be healthy and whole, but they are working against His purposes. For instance, if the doctor tells you to cut down on red meat but you continue to eat it often, eventually you may pay the price with your health through heart problems and other types of diseases. You are sick not because of a demonic attack but because you did not heed wisdom. The dilemma that separates many from healthy lives is their own unwillingness to cooperate with sound advice. God works in various ways to make us whole. So, whether it is through medical intervention or direct, divine intervention, we must act wisely to receive our healing.

Do your attitude and environment need to change? If Jesus were to walk up to you and ask, "Do you want to be healed?" what would you say? If the answer is yes, then trust God, make sure your environment is in keeping with His Word and ways, and move forward in Him.

After he was healed, the man was compelled by his deliverance to go to the temple. Nobody told him to go to the temple, but after coming in contact with Jesus, he was drawn to a holy place. Deliverance should always lead you to worship and thanksgiving. If you can stop being angry or complacent in your condition, God has a miracle waiting for you, and He wants you to use your deliverance as a testament to His goodness and power.

Allowing the Sinful Nature to Rule

When I had the revelations of hell, Jesus warned me, "On this journey, you're sometimes going to think that I have left you, but I haven't; you just won't be able to see Me." How many times have you felt as if God has left you, only to realize that He was standing right beside you all along? Just because you cannot see God does not mean that He has left you or forsaken you. *"For He Himself has said, 'I will never leave you nor forsake you'"* (Hebrews 13:5). We can rely on the security of His love while we are undergoing difficulties in life. *"We know and rely on the love God has for us"* (1 John 4:16 NIV).

Spiritual wholeness is necessary for us to become exemplary servants for the kingdom of God. This doesn't mean that we won't run across some hindrances or that we won't struggle against the sinful nature. However, through it all, the Lord will guide us from harm's way and lead us back onto the path of righteousness for the sake of His name. (See Psalm 23:3.) As we continue to reject the sinful nature and return to God, we will remain close to Him, but if we give in to the desires of the sinful nature, we will drift away and not remain focused on Him as our Healer.

The Lord will guide us from harm's way and lead us back onto the path of righteousness for the sake of His name.

Have you have lost your passion for God so that you are no longer focused on the Source of your healing? Then you will continue to be disappointed. You cannot obtain a different result by doing the same thing. Bishop Bloomer gives these insights about staying close to God our Healer:

"Although I was raised in an environment where alcohol was prevalent, I was also raised to fear God. Therefore, when I finally made an earnest commitment to serve Him wholeheartedly, my fear of Him is what always checked my spirit and kept me in line. This is not to say that I haven't made mistakes, but the reverential fear of God was the main ingredient in maintaining my spiritual sobriety and receiving deliverance through God. Consequently, I cannot do wrong without feeling the convicting power of God.

"Unfortunately, some spiritual leaders have come on the scene who minister out of zeal but who lack a strong and deep relationship with God. As a result, instead of correcting their wrongs and seeking healing in areas where they are weak, they make excuses for them. Years ago, when my friends and I were new in Christ, and we messed up, we knew that we were wrong. It bothered us, and we could find no peace until our relationships with God were restored.

"Though our spirits were willing, our flesh was weak. (See, for example, Matthew 26:41.) We never lost sight of our relationships with God in our times of weakness, yet we struggled in the midst of the war going on between our spirits and our flesh. As Paul wrote, *'For in my inner being I delight in God's law; but I see another law at work in the members of my body, waging war against the law of my mind and making me a prisoner of the law of sin at work within my members'* (Romans 7:22–23 NIV).

"We would ask for forgiveness and recommit to following God while our flesh tugged at us to return to our sinful ways. As we grew spiritually, we learned that the power of the Holy Spirit and personal discipline enable us to keep the flesh under control.

"Again, the apostle Paul explains our spiritual struggle clearly in the book of Romans:

We know that the law is spiritual; but I am unspiritual, sold as a slave to sin. I do not understand what I do. For what I want to do I do not do, but what I hate I do. (Romans 7:14–15 NIV)

"Here we see that when the unspiritual nature, or *'sinful nature'* (Romans 7:5 NIV), tries to conform to spiritual laws by its own efforts, it can't do it. When we are born again, we receive a new spiritual nature from God that is not ruled or controlled by sin. Yet the sinful nature remains inside us until we die, so that there is an ongoing battle for supremacy. Sometimes, we give in to the sinful nature and allow it to rule over the spiritual nature. When our sinful natures rule, we do things that go against our confession of faith. We may find ourselves showing up at places where we shouldn't be going and doing things that we shouldn't be doing.

> *And if I do what I do not want to do, I agree that the law is good. As it is, it is no longer I myself who do it, but it is sin living in me. I know that nothing good lives in me, that is, in my sinful nature. For I have the desire to do what is good, but I cannot carry it out. For what I do is not the good I want to do; no, the evil I do not want to do—this I keep on doing. Now if I do what I do not want to do, it is no longer I who do it, but it is sin living in me that does it.*   (verses 16–20 NIV)

"Paul said that *'nothing good lives'* in his sinful nature. He found himself wanting to do good, but he could not seem to figure out how to do so based solely upon his own will because he was influenced by the sinful nature, which wanted to do the opposite. The good that he attempted to do, he continued to fail at doing; but the evil from which he wanted to refrain, he found himself continuing to do. His conclusion was that *'it is no longer I who do it, but it is sin living in me that does it.'* The sinful nature committed these sinful acts against his will.

> *So I find this law at work: When I want to do good, evil is right there with me. For in my inner being I delight in God's law; but I see another law at work in the members of my body, waging war against the law of my mind and making me a prisoner of the law of sin at work within my members. What a wretched man I am! Who will rescue me from this body of death? Thanks be to God—through Jesus Christ our Lord!*

So then, I myself in my mind am a slave to God's law,
but in the sinful nature a slave to the law of sin.
(verses 21–25 NIV)

"In these final verses, Paul concluded that although the sinful nature was present within him, there was a spiritual nature within, as well, which he had received through Christ: *'For in my inner being I delight in God's law'* (verse 22). He made a conscious decision to allow the Spirit of God to deliver his *'wretched man'* from its sinful nature. With his renewed spirit and mind, he could now successfully serve God, even though his flesh continually sought *'the law of sin.'* He knew that one day, he would live completely in the freedom that Christ had won for him when the sinful nature would be gone forever in his resurrected body.

"Paul realized that without discipline, it is impossible to serve God.

Do you not know that those who run in a race all run,
but one receives the prize? Run in such a way that you
may obtain it. And everyone who competes for the prize
is temperate in all things. Now they do it to obtain a
perishable crown, but we for an imperishable crown.
Therefore I run thus: not with uncertainty. Thus I fight:
*not as one who beats the air. But **I discipline my body***
and bring it into subjection, lest, when I have preached
to others, I myself should become disqualified.
(1 Corinthians 9:24–27, emphasis added)

"Discipline and growth in God is a process. We must be patient with this process and not give up. My mother takes care of children. One little boy was trying to walk, and every time the little boy would stumble, his mother would grab him and put him in the walker. Finally, my mother told the little boy's mom, 'Your son is never going to learn to walk if you keep putting him in that walker.'

"The mother replied, 'I don't want him to fall and bump his head.'

"'The only way he is going to get comfortable in standing is by getting comfortable in falling.'

"I found that to be a very valid point. The only way we can learn to stand in Christ is by taking the initiative to recover after we've fallen. As babies in the natural, we crawl, stagger, stumble, fall, get up, and eventually walk. The mother of the little boy had allowed her own fears and traumas to stunt the child's growth. How many times have we allowed our own idiosyncrasies and tragedies to hinder our growth and prevent us from being a strong example to others?

"When I asked my mother where she learned this, she simply responded, 'I've raised nine kids. I'm an expert at this.' She then pointed out another child in the room who was just learning to walk but had become accustomed to cushioning his own fall. As soon as the child realized that he was stumbling, he'd lift both hands, brace himself, and fall comfortably on his bottom. He'd then get up and go back to playing all over again.

"God doesn't want us to fall by sinning, but He knows that as long as we are on this earth, we will make mistakes and sometimes sin. Far too many people are falling and allowing themselves to self-destruct in the process.

"First, they are not relying on God's Spirit for strength and a 'way of escape' from temptation.

Let him who thinks he stands take heed lest he fall. No temptation has overtaken you except such as is common to man; but God is faithful, who will not allow you to be tempted beyond what you are able, but with the temptation will also make the way of escape, that you may be able to bear it. (1 Corinthians 10:12–13)

"Second, they are not quickly coming to God for forgiveness after they sin.

If we confess our sins, He is faithful and just to forgive us our sins and to cleanse us from all unrighteousness. (1 John 1:9)

My little children, these things I write to you, so that you may not sin. And if anyone sins, we have an Advocate with the Father, Jesus Christ the righteous. And He Himself is the propitiation for our sins, and not for ours only but also for the whole world. (1 John 2:1–2)

God knows how to lift you from every difficult fall if you will only call upon Him earnestly for forgiveness and help.

"When you ask God to have mercy on you, it is because you did something that you knew was wrong. The only way to restoration is through God's grace and mercy in Jesus Christ. God knows how to lift you from every difficult fall if you will only call upon Him earnestly for forgiveness and help instead of running away from Him. He inclines His ear to us and hears our cries. He brings us up out of the 'horrible pits' (see Psalm 40:1–2), but if our mind-sets do not change, there can be no real healing."

Walk in the Spirit

We must learn to allow our new spiritual natures, under the control of the Holy Spirit, to direct our lives. Then the sinful nature will not reign in us, and we can maintain unclouded relationships with God. In this way, we can remain focused in faith on the Source of our healing—spiritually, mentally, emotionally, and physically.

From the beginning God chose you to be saved through the sanctifying work of the Spirit and through belief in the truth. He called you to this through our gospel, that you might share in the glory of our Lord Jesus Christ. So then, brothers, stand firm and hold to the teachings we passed on to you, whether by word of mouth or by letter. (2 Thessalonians 2:13–15 NIV)

There is therefore now no condemnation to those who are in Christ Jesus, who do not walk according to the flesh, but according to the Spirit. For the law of the Spirit of life in Christ Jesus has made me free from the law of sin and death. For what the law could not do in that it was weak through the flesh, God did by sending His own Son in the likeness of sinful flesh, on account of sin: He condemned sin in the flesh, that the righteous requirement of the law might be fulfilled in us who do not walk according to the flesh but according to the Spirit. For those who live according to the flesh set their minds on the things of the flesh, but those who live according to the Spirit, the things of the Spirit. For to be carnally minded is death, but to be spiritually minded is life and peace. Because the carnal mind is enmity against God; for it is not subject to the law of

God, nor indeed can be. So then, those who are in the flesh cannot please God. But you are not in the flesh but in the Spirit, if indeed the Spirit of God dwells in you. Now if anyone does not have the Spirit of Christ, he is not His. And if Christ is in you, the body is dead because of sin, but the Spirit is life because of righteousness. But if the Spirit of Him who raised Jesus from the dead dwells in you, He who raised Christ from the dead will also give life to your mortal bodies through His Spirit who dwells in you. Therefore, brethren, we are debtors; not to the flesh, to live according to the flesh. For if you live according to the flesh you will die; but if by the Spirit you put to death the deeds of the body, you will live. (Romans 8:1–13)

Walk in the Spirit, and you shall not fulfill the lust of the flesh. For the flesh lusts against the Spirit, and the Spirit against the flesh; and these are contrary to one another, so that you do not do the things that you wish....But the fruit of the Spirit is love, joy, peace, longsuffering, kindness, goodness, faithfulness, gentleness, self-control. Against such there is no law. And those who are Christ's have crucified the flesh with its passions and desires. If we live in the Spirit, let us also walk in the Spirit. (Galatians 5:16–17, 22–25)

Chapter 9

PERSEVERING FOR YOUR HEALING
Keys to Receiving a Breakthrough
by George Bloomer

"You have persevered and have patience, and have labored for My name's sake and have not become weary."
—Revelation 2:3

The ability to persevere is a key to receiving healing. Someone who perseveres does not give up easily. James wrote, *"Indeed we count them blessed who endure. You have heard of the perseverance of Job and seen the end intended by the Lord; that the Lord is very compassionate and merciful"* (James 5:11). To illustrate the quality of perseverance, let us look at the account of a healing Jesus performed in the city of Capernaum.

The area in and around Capernaum was known to those in Galilee and beyond as a place where Jesus performed great healings and supernatural manifestations. (See, for example, Matthew 4:13–25; Mark 1:21–34.) In Mark 2, we read that Jesus returned to the house in which He was staying in Capernaum after preaching, casting out demons, and healing a leper in nearby towns. When the word got out that He was there, the house filled with people.

> And again He entered Capernaum after some days, and it was heard that He was in the house. Immediately many gathered together, so that there was no longer room to receive them, not even near the door. And He preached the word to them.   (Mark 2:1–2)

Desperate to get to Jesus, some in the crowd went to great extremes to reach Him on behalf of one who was sick:

> Then they came to Him, bringing a paralytic who was carried by four men. And when they could not come near Him because of the crowd, they uncovered the roof where He was. So when they had broken through, they let down the bed on which the paralytic was lying.   (verses 3–4)

The Necessity of Spiritual Support

Friends Who Don't Give Up

Four individuals came carrying a man who was paralyzed, determined to get him to Jesus to be healed. This man had lost his ability to control his own movements; his body had weakened, and Jesus was his only hope. Many of us are suffering from types of spiritual and emotional paralysis. Perhaps the enemy played with your mind, and you found yourself doing things that almost seemed out of your control. The devil wants to stop you from being strong in the Lord. He may manipulate your environment to cause havoc in your life. Yet when you are surrounded by concerned, spiritual friends, like those depicted in the account of the paralytic who was lowered from the roof to Jesus, you receive spiritual support to help fight such demonic influences. This man's friends knew that he was going through a storm from which only Jesus could set him free.

When you are surrounded by concerned, spiritual friends, you receive spiritual support to help fight demonic influences.

These friends had such compassion that not only did they carry this man to the location, but they also went to the extreme of pulling off the roof so they could lower him down through it. They understood the concept of Matthew 11:12: "*The kingdom of heaven suffers violence, and the violent take it by force.*" I imagine that the state of mind of these friends and of the paralyzed man was one of great desperation or determination—or both. Again, the paralyzed man thankfully had friends who did not give up on him.

Difficulties may happen in your life so that God can get the glory. Your trial can seem so intense that you begin to question, "God, why are You allowing me to go through this? Why have You left me in this predicament!" Sometimes, it's the little distractions that block us from receiving our miracles. When crises come, they may arrive in clusters, threatening to break us down and ultimately destroy our faith in God. Yet, as we persevere in faith and love, God will be glorified in the end. Gain strength from the support of those who are committed to your healing or deliverance, even when you feel like giving up.

The Bible says that the friends took the paralyzed man to the roof and began uncovering it and breaking it up so they could get him inside. Some miracles don't take place until we uncover things and break them up so that the enemy will never be able to use them against us again.

This group of friends would not be deterred or convinced to turn back. Again, they went to extreme measures. *"When Jesus saw their faith, He said to the paralytic, 'Son, your sins are forgiven you....I say to you, arise, take up your bed, and go to your house'"* (Mark 2:5, 11). Jesus was touched by the faith of those who were carrying the man. Their faith had helped to make him whole. Do you have anyone in your life who refuses to give up on you regardless of how bad things look?

My mother was such a person in my life. As a young teen running the streets of Brooklyn, New York, I'd acquired a drug habit that almost took my life. One night, I was out with a group of "friends" and accidentally overdosed. They threw me into the car, drove me to the hospital, dumped me at the front door, and sped off into the night. By the grace and mercy of God, a doctor came by and quickly rushed me into the ER. My pulse was sinking and I was dying. By the time my mother reached the hospital, my heart had stopped, and the doctors were working frantically to bring me back to life.

Then, the strangest thing happened. Although by medical standards I was dead, I could hear my mother screaming at me to wake up. I appeared to be hovering in the room, yet I could see my lifeless form lying on the hospital bed. My mother was screaming, "George Gary! Get up!" Then she began crying out to God to raise me up from the bed. And that is exactly what God did. My heart began pumping again, and the doctors were able to get a pulse. God had given me a second chance at life.

My mother showed the same tenacity and perseverance with God as the woman of Shunem. (See 2 Kings 4:8–37.) Despite the fact that her son had died, she believed that God would work through the prophet Elisha to raise him up, and she said in faith, *"It is well"* (verse 26).

Believers Who Pray for Spiritual Strength

I have also benefited from the spiritual support of believers whom I didn't even know. For example, some time ago, I was not feeling as close to God as I once had because I was going through one crisis after another and didn't see any relief in sight. I went to Tampa, Florida, to preach in a crusade, and while I was preaching, I kept noticing a lady sitting in the middle of the church and rocking back and forth. After the service was over, I approached her and said, "I noticed that through the whole service, you were rocking back and forth and speaking in tongues." She explained, "Son, I was praying for you to get a breakthrough. I know it's hard to stand up there and deliver a word to people and have to forget about your own problems while trying to deliver someone else. And I saw how the people were pulling on your spirit, but I didn't see anyone who was praying for you."

Pastors and other spiritual leaders need the spiritual support of believers.

It is vital to pray for pastors and other spiritual leaders. An unfortunate but growing trend in the church is that people are going to meetings mainly to see "superstars." They have become so intrigued with the celebrity attached to leaders that they fail to see the call of God upon the lives of preachers and evangelists to lead people to Jesus. The church is losing its spiritual zeal to pray and see the full manifestations of God. We no longer pray as we once did, nor do we diligently seek the face of God until His presence captures the entire atmosphere of a meeting.

We must remember that our leaders are spiritual vessels who are also made of flesh and blood. Unless they maintain the proper focus, they are subject to failure, just as anyone else is. They need the spiritual support of their congregations and other believers. Yet if a leader makes a mistake or commits a moral failure, what do members of the congregation and others often do? They gossip about it through e-mails, text messages, or phone calls, and they condemn the leader instead of getting on their knees and asking God to restore him or her, as His Word instructs us to do: *"Brethren, if a man is overtaken in any trespass, you who are spiritual restore such a one in a spirit of gentleness, considering yourself lest you also be tempted. Bear one another's burdens, and so fulfill the law of Christ"* (Galatians 6:1–2).

Such leaders may have prayed diligently for people and their families until they received the healings they sought, but when they found themselves in need of prayer, these people were nowhere to be found. The leaders were treated as if they had a contagious disease.

Jesus told the story of a man who was ambushed while traveling: *"A certain man went down from Jerusalem to Jericho, and fell among thieves, who stripped him of his clothing, wounded him, and departed, leaving him half dead"* (Luke 10:30). The man was stripped not only of his material possessions but also of his dignity. Imagine leaving the lofty, well-lit streets of Jerusalem only to find yourself wallowing helplessly in the dirty, darkened streets of Jericho, having lost in a matter of minutes what may have taken years for you to accumulate. When people find themselves in their darkest hours and their most vulnerable states, the last thing they need is for people to look down on them and criticize them. Yet this is what happened in the story of the man who was attacked by thieves. *"Now by chance a certain priest came down that road. And when he saw him, he passed by on the other side. Likewise a Levite, when he arrived at the place, came and looked, and passed by on the other side"* (Luke 10:31–32). It took a Samaritan—with whom Jews of the day normally did not associate—to have mercy on the man and help him:

> *But a certain Samaritan, as he journeyed, came where he was. And when he saw him, he had compassion. So he went to him and bandaged his wounds, pouring on oil and wine; and he set him on his own animal, brought him to an inn, and took care of him.*
>
> (verses 33–34)

There are always opportunistic individuals waiting for leaders to fall in order to bask in their demise. Yet, sometimes, God will use a person's failure to strengthen him or her and cause that person to grow spiritually so he or she may serve Him to an even greater degree.

Anytime God gives you an opportunity to tell your testimony, don't just share the "pretty" side of it; be willing to share your "paralytic" experiences, too. When you cover up your sin, it permits the devil to continue raising havoc in your life. Yet when you confess your sins to God, then you strip the demonic kingdom of its power to hold you captive to your sins. When you have been restored by God and you testify of your own free will about your failings as well as your victories, you remove the stinger from the devil's attack against you. This is when the healing can truly begin. And this is when ministry to others can occur.

Of course, this is not to suggest that people should purposefully "fall" so that they can be used by God. As the apostle Paul wrote, *"What shall we say then? Shall we continue in sin that grace may abound? Certainly not! How shall we who died to sin live any longer in it?"* (Romans 6:1–2). While we may fall into sin, we should no longer make a practice of it.

We usually grow in stages instead of all at once, and God sometimes leaves us with a "limp" from our prior failures, at least for a time. This is so that there's evidence of where we have been and how far we have come. Many people who have gone through pure "hell" have learned how to praise God in the midst of their pain and in the midst of their storms. How awesome it is for someone who has been severely attacked by the devil to be able to say to him, "You sent enemies down to rob me and to strip me of my dignity, and then you left me for dead. Yet, after it was over, I stood up in Christ, and I'm still standing!"

When was the last time you prayed and fasted on behalf of someone else who was in desperate spiritual, emotional, or physical need? Sometimes, God can't speak to us because our spiritual bellies are too full to hear what He is saying or to see what He is showing us.

A woman came into my office and asked for prayer for her grandchild, who was experiencing strange occurrences in the home. "Bishop," she said, "I'm having a problem with my grandbaby, who is seeing demons and spirits. There's a ghost in the house; there are chills all over the house, and the house is beginning to smell." I admitted to her, "I don't know what this is. But I believe that if we pray and fast, God will give us a revelation."

Again, we may need a revelation from God, but we can't receive it because our spiritual, mental, emotional, and physical bellies are filled with too much "junk food." This woman and I prayed and fasted and sought the face of God regarding her grandchild. We found out that the little girl was being attacked by witches in her school. If you remain persistent, God will give you the revelation you need to be set free or to help set others free. Sometimes, people may have "given place" to the devil (see Ephesians 4:27) in certain areas of their lives, and this begins to manifest as sickness. You have to be in close relationship with God and spiritually attuned in order to see past the devil's smoke screens, rebuke him, and plead the blood of Jesus in the lives of these people so they may be set free.

God will give you the revelation you need to be set free or to help set others free.

Go to the Source

The paralytic man's friends had carried him to meet his miracle, and from that point, Jesus "carried" him on to healing.

When Jesus saw their faith, He said to the paralytic, "Son, your sins are forgiven you." And some of the scribes were sitting there and reasoning in their hearts, "Why does this Man speak blasphemies like this? Who can forgive sins but God alone?" But immediately, when Jesus perceived in His spirit that they reasoned thus within themselves, He said to them, "Why do you reason about these things in your hearts? Which is easier, to say to the paralytic, 'Your sins are forgiven you,' or to say, 'Arise, take up your bed and walk'? But that you may know that the Son of Man has power on earth to forgive sins"; He said to the paralytic, "I say to you, arise, take up your bed, and go to your house." Immediately he arose, took up the bed, and went out in the presence of them all, so that all were amazed and glorified God, saying, "We never saw anything like this!" (Mark 2:5–12)

Jesus used the man's illness to make a point to the on-lookers of the goodness and greatness of God. The same applies to your dilemmas and crises in life: Jesus takes what the devil meant for evil and uses it for your good. (See Genesis 50:20.) He is using your life to make a point to unbelievers and believers alike. You may not always enjoy the process because He is the only One who knows the outcome as you are going through your problem. You may often feel very lonely and neglected, asking yourself, *Am I going to be able to live to see the point that Jesus is trying to make through my life?* Just remember that there are some things going on in your life from which no one can deliver you but Jesus. And you must make every effort to reach out to Him, despite how you feel.

Note that the religious leaders had a problem with the paralytic's healing. As long as he was paralyzed, they were fine with his condition, but as soon as Jesus healed him, they protested. Instead of honoring Jesus, they found fault with Him. "Religious" people will not always encour-age you to seek healing, and they may not be happy when you do receive it, so you must take your requests straight to Jesus—the Source of your healing. Regardless of the problem, take it to Jesus. Learn to praise God and continue leaning on Him no matter what you are going through.

I am not one who gets sick often, but at one point, for two years in a row, I contracted the flu during "flu season." Even though I took lots of vitamin C and made sure I bundled up properly, surprisingly, I ended up with bad cases of the flu. One year, when I was in bed, recovering, I began to feel strong enough to get up and start moving around. But when I got up, I became so overwhelmed that I was instantly forced to lie back down. I was in bed for three days. Even after regaining my strength, I was left with a nagging cough that lasted for about three months. I went back and forth to various doctors who explained to me that I was suffering from a strange strain of the flu that many had contracted. They gave me vitamin C and antibiotics until the third doctor finally admitted, "You're just going to have to wait this one out."

That situation revealed to me that we will go through many things in life that will require us to hold on to God as we wait things out. We cannot give up or lose hope, but we must believe that He is able to bring us through any crisis or dilemma that threatens to incapacitate us. Perhaps you are now in a waiting-it-out position.

Once, I got on a plane to travel to Florida to preach, but when the plane reached about thirty thousand feet, the air traffic control tower advised the pilot to turn the plane around. The skies blackened, and we were routed to New York instead of Florida. The following day, we saw on the news that many houses in Florida had been flattened by the storm—they were turned to mere rubble. The roof had been completely torn off the church where I had been scheduled to preach. The winds had actually picked up a car and tossed it in front of the altar inside the church!

God often buffers us to keep us from feeling the complete ferocity of Satan's demonic attacks.

We may have no idea of the spiritual intensity of the storms we are going through in life because God often buffers us to keep us from feeling the complete ferocity of Satan's demonic attacks. The pastor of the church had been out of town, and he had been on his way back home when his plane was also rerouted. The only person in his home at the time of the storm was his housekeeper. She had been told earlier that day that the area was being evacuated, but she'd decided to stay. She said that when the storm came, it was so fierce that it tore up the porch, shattered the windows, and suctioned every bit of water out of the pool.

The housekeeper ran into the pastor's room and hid beneath the bed. She cried out to God, "Lord, I don't have anybody to touch and agree with." It was then that she noticed a pair of the pastor's shoes. She placed both hands on the shoes and began to pray, "Father, I set myself in agreement with the shoes that the man of God walks in...." The pastor of the church later took me to see the damage to his home, which had been completely demolished—except for one room: the bedroom where the housekeeper had been praying.

A storm will come in your life that only God can get you through. When the storm is over, you will have a story to tell others about His power to deliver. The housekeeper reported that following the storm, she slept all night long, holding on to the man of God's shoes.

The church was rebuilt, and, months later, I went there to preach. While I was there, I ran into her. She shared with me that she had been taught by her pastor always to have faith in God, regardless of the storm or circumstance. No matter what you are going through, have faith in God and hold on to Him.

Don't Give Up at the Brink of Receiving

Spiritual perseverance is key. Many times, we give up right at the brink of receiving what we need from God. Who knows the mind of God and His timing? For as soon as we feel as if we have God all figured out, He acts in a way that is different from the method we expected. *"Trust in the* LORD *with all your heart, and lean not on your own understanding; in all your ways acknowledge Him, and He shall direct your paths"* (Proverbs 3:5–6). God will direct the paths of those who continue to trust Him during both the good and bad times in life. We all have had times when we did not feel like praying or seeking the face of God, but, normally, those are the times during which we need to seek Him the most.

God will direct the paths of those who continue to trust Him during both the good and bad times in life.

Do you need a breakthrough today? Persevere in faith and prayer, and God will bring you out!

Whatever you need healing for—your body, your mind, your family, your finances, or anything else—entrust it to

Your heavenly Father. Let's agree together in prayer for a breakthrough:

> Father, I agree with those who are reading this book today to receive the healing and deliverance they need. I pray that their faith will rise as never before. Despite how difficult things might seem, may Your Spirit meet them right where they are to bring them comfort and strength. I pray that Your anointing will fill every corner of their beings. I decree by the authority of Jesus that the devil cannot keep them bound. Satan, take your hands off God's property! I bind demons and release victory in the name of Christ. I curse addictions and release deliverance right now, in Jesus' name. Touch them, Father God, from the tops of their heads to the soles of their feet. Bring breakthroughs and release to every person who is right now putting his or her faith in you. Amen.

God has carried you this far, and He has promised to deliver you. Worship and praise Him. Allow your praises to create the atmosphere for your deliverance. Persevere for your healing.

> *Therefore humble yourselves under the mighty hand of God, that He may exalt you in due time, casting all your care upon Him, for He cares for you. Be sober, be vigilant; because your adversary the devil walks about like a roaring lion, seeking whom he may devour. Resist him, steadfast in the faith, knowing that the same sufferings are experienced by your brotherhood in the world. May the God of all grace, who called us to His*

eternal glory by Christ Jesus, after you have suffered a while, perfect, establish, strengthen, and settle you. To Him be the glory and the dominion forever and ever. Amen.   (1 Peter 5:6–11)

Chapter 10

MINISTERING HEALING TO OTHERS

*"And these signs will follow those who believe:
In My name they will cast out demons; they will speak with
new tongues; they will take up serpents; and if they drink
anything deadly, it will by no means hurt them; they will lay
hands on the sick, and they will recover."*
—Mark 16:17–18

When Jesus first sent out His twelve disciples to minister to people, He said, *"Heal the sick, cleanse the lepers, raise the dead, cast out demons. **Freely you have received, freely give**"* (Matthew 10:8, emphasis added). The same principle applies to us today. As we have received, we are to give freely. God has called us to minister to others as He has ministered to us.

> *If you have any encouragement from being united with Christ, if any comfort from his love, if any fellowship with the Spirit, if any tenderness and compassion, then make my joy complete by being like-minded, having the same love, being one in spirit and purpose. Do nothing out of selfish ambition or vain conceit, but in humility consider others better than*

173

yourselves. Each of you should look not only to your own interests, but also to the interests of others.
(Philippians 2:1–4 NIV)

When you have returned to Me, strengthen your brethren. (Luke 22:32)

As we minister **spiritual healing** to others, we are ambassadors of reconciliation:

[God] has reconciled us to Himself through Jesus Christ, and has given us the ministry of reconciliation, that is, that God was in Christ reconciling the world to Himself, not imputing their trespasses to them, and has committed to us the word of reconciliation. Now then, we are ambassadors for Christ, as though God were pleading through us. (2 Corinthians 5:18–20)

Brethren, if a man is overtaken in any trespass, you who are spiritual restore such a one in a spirit of gentleness, considering yourself lest you also be tempted. Bear one another's burdens, and so fulfill the law of Christ. (Galatians 6:1–2)

As we minister **healing for the soul**, we reflect the character of God:

Be kind to one another, tenderhearted, forgiving one another, just as God in Christ forgave you.
(Ephesians 4:32)

Warn those who are idle, encourage the timid, help the weak, be patient with everyone.
(1 Thessalonians 5:14 NIV)

As we minister **healing for the body,** we demonstrate the power of God:

> *Grant to Your servants that with all boldness they may speak Your word, by stretching out Your hand to heal, and that signs and wonders may be done through the name of Your holy Servant Jesus.* (Acts 4:29–30)

> *I have reason to glory in Christ Jesus in the things which pertain to God. For I will not dare to speak of any of those things which Christ has not accomplished through me, in word and deed, to make the Gentiles obedient; in mighty signs and wonders, by the power of the Spirit of God.* (Romans 15:17–19)

Let Your Light Shine

There are people whom God will place around you in order for those individuals to receive their healings. Whether it is spiritual, mental, emotional, or physical healing, we are to pray for these people and sow God's Word and compassionate acts into their lives. We are not to condemn them because of their lack of knowledge or unbelief, but rather to bring love and healing. The Bible says that if you do right by people, they will see your good works and glorify God because they will see Him in you. *"Let your light so shine before men, that they may see your good works and glorify your Father in heaven"* (Matthew 5:16). We allow people to see God in us by doing what Jesus commands us to do for

If you do right by people, they will see your good works and glorify God because they will see Him in you.

others. *"All the law is fulfilled in one word, even in this: 'You shall love your neighbor as yourself'"* (Galatians 5:14). People today want to see our works, not just hear us speak about Jesus the Savior. They don't always understand the whole spiritual phenomenon. If they hear your miraculous testimony but then see you acting in a way that contradicts the love of God that you have spoken about, it will confuse them and will likely turn them away.

Follow the example of Jesus. Unlike many of us, after Jesus ministered to people, He did not wait around for a pat on the back. He simply went on to perform other great miracles and spread the goodness of God. When you have the nature of Jesus, you don't always have tell everyone what you do for others; you just do it.

Minister according to the Gift of God

Jesus is *"King of kings and Lord of lords"* (1 Timothy 6:15), and He is impacting our lives today in remarkable ways. I go to many jails—women's prisons, men's prisons, juvenile detention centers—visiting prisoners and preaching on hell, and three or four hundred will often be saved at once. Sadly, the juveniles are the most rebellious. The world today really must turn to the cross of Jesus for salvation, healing, and deliverance.

My ministry is due to the power and calling of the Lord Jesus. I was an ordinary homemaker, and I never dreamed that I would be doing what I am doing today. It is all through obedience to God—acting on what He has called me to do. We are to obey Him, regardless of what our current situation in life is and no matter what we think we are capable of.

Many times when I am preaching, the Lord will send an angel to stand beside the person who is about to get a healing. When I see this, I immediately go to this person and begin praying for him or her. Every time I am obedient to God, He always heals. And when you are obedient to Him, He will do the same.

The manifestation of the gifts of God are diverse, but they all work for the same purpose—that the glory of God might be fulfilled.

> *There are diversities of gifts, but the same Spirit. There are differences of ministries, but the same Lord. And there are diversities of activities, but it is the same God who works all in all. But the manifestation of the Spirit is given to each one for the profit of all.*
> (1 Corinthians 12:4–7)

Whatever gift God gives you is to be used to set others free. When He sends us to do His work, we can't waste time questioning Him in disbelief. We cannot hold back our gifts. The devil does not want us to use those gifts because he knows that the anointing will be released and many will be saved for the Lord and healed of their infirmities. When God gives you overcoming power, you become as bold as a lion and are no longer intimidated by people—or the enemy.

When God gives you overcoming power, you are no longer intimidated by people—or the enemy.

You should never underestimate God. When He wants to give you a gift, not only should you receive it, but you should also make sure that you use it for His glory.

Years ago, when I first started my ministry, my children were little, so I didn't go out ministering a lot. But I was in a wonderful church, and the pastor said there was a child about a year and a half old who was in the hospital. They wanted some of us to go and pray. He was supposed to have surgery in a day or so.

Early the next morning, the Lord said to me, *Get up and go to the hospital to the children's floor.* So I obeyed Him. I went to the waiting room in the children's hospital. Back then, there wasn't the security that we have today in hospitals, and you could go to the hospital and pray for people.

I didn't know what room the baby was in, but the Lord showed me a corridor He wanted me to walk down. He said, *I'm going to lead you right to the baby.* I went down the corridor, and in one room, I saw a little boy lying in a bed that had a top on it so that the child couldn't get out. There was a plaque with his name on it.

The baby was crying. I laid my hands on his stomach and began praying for him in the Holy Spirit, and the baby calmed down. A nurse came by, and I told her, "I'm just praying for the baby." She said, "That's good. He really needs prayer." After praying, I returned home.

A friend of mine had been at the hospital that same day, and she called to share with me a strange occurrence that had happened while she was there. "They'd brought in a young autistic boy who'd swallowed a bedspring," she said. "They were about to operate on him, and I prayed that they wouldn't have to operate because of the mental state that he was already in. They went to operate on him and noticed that he was no longer crying, so they X-rayed him again and saw that the bedspring was gone." I knew this was the same child whom I'd laid hands on earlier that day. Thank God that He did not show me what his ailment was because I probably would have hesitated to lay my hands on his stomach for fear of hurting him. God knows exactly what to reveal to us and at what time in order for His will to be fulfilled.

God can do anything! You have to believe in God and believe that He is still the worker of miracles. It is God doing the healing and not ourselves. When we remember that, it removes the pressure from us and places the glory of the miraculous where it belongs—on Him.

Press On!

We should *"not grow weary in doing good"* (2 Thessalonians 3:13), because God is always at work behind the scenes. As He uses us to bless others, He is blessing us in the process. We may not always be able to see what God is doing, but He is working things out on our behalf. If we just continue to keep the faith and not give up, we will see the manifestation of our commitment to Him working through our daily lives.

As God uses us to bless others, He is blessing us in the process.

Once, I went to a church to preach, and the pastor shared with me a problem that he was having with one of the members in his church. "Mary," he said, "there is one lady who comes to me every service and asks me to pray for her. Each time, it's for a different ailment: her stomach, her eye, her toe, her head…whatever. Each service, she aggravates me and asks me to pray for her. So Mary, please pray and ask God why I have to do this." So I went in prayer for this man. As I began to pray for him, I saw a vision of him laying his hands on this woman's head. An angel was standing nearby, writing down every time he prayed for her and what he prayed about. The angel looked at me, smiled, and said, "He will get a reward in heaven for every part of her body that he prays for." When I shared this with the pastor, he began shouting for joy.

This does not mean that we are to pray for people merely to get something from God; rather, it is a reminder that we never know the plan of God and why He asks us to do things that we would not ordinarily do. As long as you are certain that you are hearing from God, you should not hesitate to act upon His instructions. *"Therefore, my beloved brethren, be steadfast, immovable, always abounding in the work of the Lord, knowing that your labor is not in vain in the Lord"* (1 Corinthians 15:58).

Once, as I was about to speak at a church, I was complaining to God about how I was being treated there. The Lord said to me, "Look on that wall." I looked at the wall next to me and saw it was a mural of the Via Dolorosa—the road of Christ's suffering. As I continued staring at that wall, the Lord said, "You've only begun to suffer. Take a good look at this." I saw in a vision the day that Christ was crucified. I saw Him carrying the cross, which was huge and very splintered. The splinters were digging into His back, and blood was all over Him. He slipped and fell on His own blood. He looked up at me, bloody and bruised, and said, "Press on." I could feel Him continuing to speak to my heart, "I died for such as this. Press on." I began to feel ashamed of how I'd been acting, and I repented before

God. Then, as I began to speak to the congregation, the anointing of the Lord fell on the entire place. The altar was filled with those who wanted to give their lives to Christ.

You have to press on, no matter what. Forget the past and shake off all the junk that is holding you back from receiving what you need from God so that you can be a blessing to others. There are many temptations today, but let it be our desire to have God in our lives and always to do the Father's will.

Thwarting the Enemy

For we do not wrestle against flesh and blood, but against principalities, against powers, against the rulers of the darkness of this age, against spiritual hosts of wickedness in the heavenly places. (Ephesians 6:12)

In order to minister, we must be aware that there is a spiritual war going on between good and evil, between the hosts of heaven and the hosts of wickedness. Evil spirits, under Satan's rule, are trying to take over heavenly places and affect our lives, and we have to drive them out in the name of Jesus. We are literally in the fight of our lives because the devil is bold. He will show up right in the midst of our prayer services and try to distract us and keep us from receiving what we need from God. But when we know where we stand in God, we cannot be defeated. We immediately recognize the enemy and eject him from the heavenly places while keeping to the truth of the Word of God. Jesus said,

When we know where we stand in God, we cannot be defeated.

Behold, I give you the authority to trample on serpents and scorpions, and over all the power of the enemy, and nothing shall by any means hurt you. Nevertheless do not rejoice in this, that the spirits are subject to you, but rather rejoice because your names are written in heaven. (Luke 10:19–20)

Once, I was ministering in Malaysia, and the Lord instructed me, *There's going to be a woman at the meeting who is a witch, and she's going to come up front and try to get you to cast the devil out of her. And she's going to do flips and break up this meeting, and the kids are going to run out the door. But don't touch her. Don't bother her; just keep on going down the line.*

"Okay, Lord, so what do You want me do?" I asked Him, because at that point I didn't know whether I should call a prayer line or not.

When the pastor asks you to pray for the people, just touch them and keep on moving down the line, the Lord answered.

Well, sure enough, before the service, the pastor came to me and said, "There's a group of young people here, and I want you to pray for them before you preach." So, I said, "Okay." As I went down the line, I just touched them and blessed each of them very quickly. Then, I came upon this woman the Lord had warned me about. She looked up at me, and her eyes suddenly rolled in opposite directions. I did as the Lord had instructed and continued down the line blessing the rest of the young people, and then I went back to my seat. All of those youths rededicated their lives to God, and God knew that the devil had been trying to prevent this.

There were several thousand people at this meeting, so security had roped off certain sections. All of a sudden, this lady broke through security, made her way to me, and said, "Didn't you see the devils in me? Aren't you even going to pray for me?" Security personnel were making their way to the stage when I responded, "No, ma'am. You can keep your devils. I'm not in the mood to cast them out."

This may sound harsh, but remember, God had already warned me of this lady's intentions, and I was determined to follow God's lead and not my own. The lady became so angry with me that she left the meeting and soon returned with all kinds of witches and warlocks. They were way in the back of the meeting place, but you could hear them. All I could say was, "Praise God, I'm going to preach hellfire and brimstone."

There were two hundred pastors there, and at the end of the meeting, one of them said to me, "Sister Mary, come on. Let's go back and see what all this commotion is about."

"I already know what it's about," I told him.

As we were walking, one of the warlocks ran up to this pastor and tried to choke him. By now, everyone had left the meeting except for a few of us. Before the warlock could choke him, something we couldn't see literally picked up the warlock and thrust him out of the way. I know that this was an angel of the Lord protecting the pastor. We thanked God! Then, those witches and warlocks began running out of the church, led by the lady who had approached me earlier.

Everything has to be done in God's timing. Sometimes, the devil sends distractions to keep the masses from receiving what they really need and desire from God. That's why, today, more than ever before, we have to be able to discern the voice of the Lord. When He says hands off, it's hands off! The Scripture says that we are not to lay hands on any man or woman hastily. (See 1 Timothy 5:22.) Rather, in all things, we are to seek the will of God. And we must know that, through Christ, God has placed the devil under our feet.

> *What is man that You are mindful of him, and the son of man that You visit him? For You have made him a little lower than the angels, and You have crowned him with glory and honor. You have made him to have dominion over the works of Your hands; You have put all things under his feet.* (Psalm 8:4–6)

> *You shall trample the wicked, for they shall be ashes under the soles of your feet.* (Malachi 4:3)

> *I want you to be wise in what is good, and simple concerning evil. And the God of peace will crush Satan under your feet shortly.* (Romans 16:19–20)

Once, a friend who had been an intercessor for me for years had cancer. The Lord came to me in the middle of the night and said, *I'm placing a special anointing on you for her. Go pray for her and I'll heal her of cancer.* That morning, there was a knock on the door, and it was another friend whom I hadn't seen in years. She had come by unexpectedly to spend the weekend with me. I invited her to go with me because I was on the way out the door.

So, off we went. The drive should have taken us only an hour and a half; but lo and behold, it took us seven hours to get there! The friend whom I'd invited to ride along with me had an upset stomach, and we wound up having to stop at several restrooms along the way to accommodate her.

When we stopped at one restroom, I prayed, "God, the devil does not want my intercessor friend to be healed. He does not want me to lay hands on her." Off we went, back onto the highway, and wouldn't you know it? I ran into construction and was stuck in bumper-to-bumper traffic for another hour with my friend in the car beside me complaining again that she had to use the restroom. "Well, get out and go to one of the little Porta-Potties that the men use," I answered in my frustration.

Finally, I got to the intercessor's home. It was after seven o'clock, and I had begun my drive that morning. I ran into the house and, without hesitating, explained to her, "Don't say a word. I have to pray for you right now!" She replied, "Oh, I know. The Lord showed me, but He also showed me that the devil didn't want you to get here." Well, I finally laid hands on her chest, and the power of God shot through her and healed her of that cancer. Praise God!

The truth that God wants me to convey to you is that through the name of Jesus, you have victory over the devil. The enemy may hit you with an attack, but he cannot stand against the light and power of the Lord.

The enemy may hit you with an attack, but he cannot stand against the light and power of the Lord.

We must be on our guard. Many times, the enemy will come when we are tired or when we have been seeking the Lord for deliverance. Once, while I was asleep in bed, I suddenly felt as if something had frozen me; I couldn't move. I was so angry that I said, "Devil, whenever I'm released from this, you're going to get it!" I began calling on the name of Jesus and repeating, "The blood of Jesus… the blood of Jesus…the blood of Jesus," and it lifted.

Then, in a vision, the Holy Spirit took my eyes over four states: Florida, Georgia, Tennessee, and West Virginia. I saw a warehouse, and God took the walls away from it so that I could see twelve people with their arms around each other, chanting. The first thing I thought was, *Well, it takes twelve devils to come against one little Christian.* Then, I saw a large snake that was trying to attack me. I began asking the Lord, "What do you want me to do?" *Rebuke it in the name of Jesus,* was His reply. So that is what I did. When I rebuked this thing, it immediately went backward and turned into a puff of smoke. Then the angels of the Lord came and drove off those who were chanting. They ran away screaming.

Later, a man who had been delivered from the occult explained to me what this vision meant. He stated that those in the occult had a hit list of people from twelve different states who were growing in the Lord. He said that they meet at least once a month and plan out how to cause certain ones a lot of heartache and grief. He explained to me that when we feel this attack, if we begin to pray in the Holy Spirit, then the Holy Spirit will protect us from those devices. Sometimes, we're so tired we don't listen. But if you anoint yourself with oil and pray and seek God, you will win. By faith, we march on to the victory line with the Lord Jesus Christ.

We have to believe that God can heal us. Just when God is about to bless us, the devil goes on his attack. So, we ask God, "Lord, why do I have to keep going through this just to get what You have for me?" We begin to doubt God and even begin to think that He no longer cares about us. We must renew our faith and press on, no matter what, because the greater One resides within us. (See 1 John 4:4.) Even when we feel so bad that the very thought of healing seems out of reach, we still have to hold on to God and believe that our healing is already manifested:

> *Now faith is the substance of things hoped for, the evidence of things not seen. For by it the elders obtained a good testimony. By faith we understand that the worlds were framed by the word of God, so that the things which are seen were not made of things which are visible.* (Hebrews 11:1–3)

Get Ready for God's Miraculous Outpouring

We don't want to miss God for any reason. Whether He gets our attention through dreams, visions, or trials, He will get our attention. God is about to rain down His righteousness upon His people. We have to get prepared for the great revival that God is about to allow us to experience upon the earth.

> *For if that first covenant had been faultless, then no place would have been sought for a second. Because finding fault with them, He says: "Behold, the days are coming, says the LORD, when I will make a new covenant with the house of Israel and with the house of Judah; not according to the covenant that I made with their fathers in the day when I took them by the hand to lead them out of the land of Egypt; because they did not continue in My covenant, and I disregarded them, says the LORD. For this is the covenant that I will make with the house of Israel after those days, says the LORD: I will put My laws in their mind and write them on their hearts; and I will be their God, and they*

shall be My people. None of them shall teach his neighbor, and none his brother, saying, 'Know the LORD,' for all shall know Me, from the least of them to the greatest of them." (Hebrews 8:7–11)

The church will go back to experiencing the supernatural healings and powerful manifestations of its early days.

The church will go back to experiencing the supernatural healings and powerful manifestations of its early days. Yet we are going to have to develop a new attitude and get ready to receive what God is about to do in the land. No longer can we have church as usual and go about the Father's business with complacency. The Father's business requires diligence. Even in our frustration, we have to exercise the patience of God and continue to believe that He knows what He is doing and that He is in control of our lives.

God loves us, and He is the One we are to look to for healing. If it were not for His provision through the blood of Jesus, we would not make it to heaven or receive our healings. Let us never give up on God nor give up on praying for one another. *"Praying always with all prayer and supplication in the Spirit, being watchful to this end with all perseverance and supplication for all the saints"* (Ephesians 6:18). We are a people who are in need of healing, and healing cannot come unless we submit ourselves to God.

Chapter 11

THE HEALING OF THE NATIONS
God's Blessings for the World
by George Bloomer

"'God will wipe away every tear from their eyes; there shall be no more death, nor sorrow, nor crying. There shall be no more pain, for the former things have passed away.' Then He who sat on the throne said, 'Behold, I make all things new.'"
—Revelation 21:4–5

Before we come to the close of our discussion on healing, we must address the necessity of healing in the context of our nations and world. Over the years, we have heard much disheartening news about the earth, which has dwindled the faith of many to a mere pulp. Where anticipation for the future once reigned in their hearts, it has now been replaced by dread. Yet God reigns, and we are never without hope. God is and always will be the One who is in control.

> [We] *rejoice in hope of the glory of God. And not only that, but we also glory in tribulations, knowing that tribulation produces perseverance; and perseverance, character; and character, hope. Now hope does not disappoint, because the love of God has been poured out*

in our hearts by the Holy Spirit who was given to us.
(Romans 5:2–5)

The nature of the world's sicknesses include such things as hatred, abuse, oppression, racial conflicts, murder, ethnic "cleansing," war, and catastrophic natural disasters. Jesus mentioned such turmoil as leading up to the magnified terrors that the world will experience before the very end of the age:

And you will hear of wars and rumors of wars. See that you are not troubled; for all these things must come to pass, but the end is not yet. For nation will rise against nation, and kingdom against kingdom. And there will be famines, pestilences, and earthquakes in various places. All these are the beginning of sorrows.
(Matthew 24:6–8)

These troubles and calamities are symptoms of a world in peril. The world is so sick that we experience such destructive weather and conditions as strong hurricanes, tsunamis, mudslides, raging wildfires, volcanic eruptions, barren land, famine, toxic air, and contaminated water. In addition to these symptoms in the physical world, we are experiencing shaky financial systems and overwhelming social and political problems. We have numerous diseases and illnesses for which researchers cannot find a cure. If we have ever needed the grace of God and His healing power, that time is now. We need healing!

There is Hope, and His name is Jesus.

There is no "pill" that planet Earth can take for its aches and pains. No radiation treatment can dissolve its cancer. It is sick; it is dying…but, again, there is Hope, and His name is Jesus.

> For the earnest expectation of the creation eagerly waits for the revealing of the sons of God. For the creation was subjected to futility, not willingly, but because of Him who subjected it in hope; because the creation itself also will be delivered from the bondage of corruption into the glorious liberty of the children of God. For we know that the whole creation groans and labors with birth pangs together until now.
>
> (Romans 8:19–22)

Pray for the Healing of the Nations

Lately, the Lord has been speaking to me in dreams. He has always dealt with me in visions and dreams, but in recent years, these have increased. In 1999, I had a series of dreams that puzzled me and boggled my mind. Many times, in the dreams, I was approached by a well-dressed man. I was also approached by angels, but there was nothing extraordinary about them; they did not have four faces, nor were they six-winged creatures with loud voices or frightening appearances. (See Isaiah 6:1–4; Revelation 4:6–8.) There were no flaming swords or shields made of iron, just men dressed in black suits. I don't know whether the Lord felt that I couldn't handle mystical things at that time or if He just wanted the angels to appear in black suits to talk to me, but the strange thing about it is that when they talked, they never moved their mouths. They communicated through telepathy—from mind to mind.

In one particular dream, I was guided by these well-dressed angels down a long, dark hallway. A light would shine only a matter of inches in front of us—perhaps a foot or two. It was like being in an underground mine and wearing a hard hat with a light attached in front to lighten the path directly in front of you. Or, it was like driving on a highway through thick fog, where high beams impair your vision so you have to use your low beams, which give you just enough light to see the reflective strips on the road. At one point, it seemed as if we were going straight. Then there were instances when it seemed as if we were spiraling, and again the way ahead was revealed to us only in increments of inches.

An unbelievable fear fell on me, and I began to question in my mind why we were here. Yet as quickly as I could think such thoughts, the angels would give me an answer. For instance, if I felt afraid, they would say, *Fear not.* If I would question in my mind, *Where are we going?* they would respond, *It will be revealed to you in time.* They read my mind and answered my questions. They monitored my emotions and calmed my fears. Still, we kept walking—up, down, straight, or in circles, we walked. It seemed to me as if we walked for a day or so, but I never got tired. It was as if I had a renewed body.

As we walked, the darkness intensified, and noises began to accompany the thick blackness: screams, moans, grunts, sounds of agony, gaspings for breath, deep exhalations, and even gagging noises. I thought to myself, *Are we in hell?* and the angel quickly answered, *Far from that.* I thought again, *Where are we?* and he responded, *It will be revealed to you in due time.* Then he said, *Look straight ahead, and look not right or left.*

Now, remember, we were in a tunnel, hallway, or cave, and it was total darkness. It was a type of blackness that

I'd never experienced before. Again, our way was still being revealed to us in increments of inches. Although I was in a dream or vision, I still experienced human reactions, and there was nothing "celestial" about me. I was a human traveling about in the spirit world. I probably never would have thought to look to my right or left if the angel had not mentioned it, but the fact that he mentioned it made me curious. I held off from looking for a while, but when I could no longer control my curiosity, I looked to my left. There, I saw hideous creatures, sicknesses, diseases, and germs. I saw cancer, AIDS, mental illness, schizophrenia, glaucoma, arthritis, Alzheimer's, and dementia. They were alive and well and feasting on humans in these chambers behind something that looked like plate glass. There was a force field around these creatures, as well as angels holding cures. The angels were looking upon these hideous sights, but they could not get to the people.

I heard the Lord say, "Pray for the healing of the nations." Then, I turned to the angels who were with me and asked them over and over again, "Did you see that? Did you see that? Did you see that?" because by the time I said the word *that*, I saw another chamber and another chamber, and before an angel could answer me, I'd seen ten to twenty chambers.

We were moving quickly, and the cave was now well lit on the sides, but it was dark in front of us and behind us. More and more, on my right and left, sicknesses and diseases were being revealed. Outside each chamber stood a weeping angel with a cure in his hand, and the Voice intensely admonished, "Pray for the healing of the nations!"

The sounds intensified—crying, hissing, gasps, screaming, hideous laughter, moaning, weeping. Then I heard what sounded like thousands of voices chanting and shouting praises to God: "I love You, Lord!" Thousands of voices were saying in concert: "There is none like You!" and "No matter what, I praise You! If You don't heal me, I'll still praise You. Holy is the Lamb. There is none like You in all of the earth!" Thousands upon thousands of chants echoed in this chamber, confronting the agony of the voices of torment. You could hear the voices of praise over the voices of agony. I asked the angel, "Where are we, and what is this place?" And he said, *We are where praises go before God is glorified by them.* It seemed as if, before God could receive glory from our praises, they had to be processed. When we can praise God in spite of what we are going through or amid hard times and difficult situations, then our praises are purified and God is worshiped.

> *When we can praise God in spite of difficult situations, then our praises are purified and God is worshiped.*

Suddenly, it seemed as if we had stopped walking but were going forward on a moving walkway, such as you find in airports. The floor beneath us carried us at a supernaturally fast speed through the tunnel, and then we stopped. We came to a vault. It looked like the huge vaults that were used by banks during the 1930s, which took at least three men to open. This vault, however, was voice activated.

We still heard the choruses of thousands of praises coupled with the cries of horror and agony, and we waited there for an angel who had the authority to open up the vault. When this angel came, he was the first "conventional-looking" angel I'd ever seen. Again, most of the times that I had seen an angel in a vision or dream, he'd been dressed in black, but this one fit the storybook description of an angel. He appeared to be between seventeen and twenty feet tall, and he had gold hair, massive arms, and huge, feathered wings. The tops of the wings were white, like the color of doves' feathers. The bottoms of the wings were dark black, similar to the appearance of pigeons' or buzzards' feathers.

As this angel moved, you could hear symphonic sounds, as if the music of heaven accompanied his appearing, and when he appeared there was no darkness and no lights. I couldn't help but think to myself, *Maybe this is Gabriel, Michael, or even Jesus in disguise.* But the angel who accompanied me turned, looked at me, and said, *None of the above.* Then, the angel with the wings, using his voice to activate the combination to the vault, said to me, *Only He who was and is and shall forever be is worthy of that type of praise.* He spoke some symphonic words, and the vault opened up. We stepped inside, and it was a forest of trees. Each tree had leaves. Written on the leaves was the word *healing* in capital letters, and under that, I saw the name of the sickness that this leaf could cure in small letters. Immediately, I realized that I was in a chamber of heaven. The trees and leaves were like the Tree of Life mentioned in the book of Revelation, whose leaves were for *"the healing of the nations"*:

> *In the middle of its street, and on either side of the river, was the tree of life, which bore twelve fruits, each tree yielding its fruit every month. The leaves of the tree were for the healing of the nations.*
>
> (Revelation 22:2)

The angel turned to me and said, *This is what God wants us to pray for: that His will be done in the earth even as it is done in heaven.* Jesus instructed us to pray the same in the

Lord's Prayer. (See Matthew 6:10; Luke 11:2.) God's will is that we should prosper and be in health, just as our souls prosper. (See 3 John 1:2.)

Preparing for Difficult Times

As we pray for the healing of the nations, we must keep close to God and apply His wisdom for the difficult times in which we live. Early in 2004—before the housing and prime mortgage crises, before banks began to fail, and before the high gasoline prices of 2008—the Lord began to minister to me about our failing economy in the form of a series of dreams.

In one dream, I visited an ant colony, where worker ants and soldier ants were all summoned to the throne room of the queen. Upon entering the throne room, I noticed that there were queens at war with one another for the throne. The ant kingdom was in complete disarray; it was pure anarchy, and the food supplies were low. I awoke from the dream at 2:45 a.m., totally confused and afraid—knowing little to nothing about ants. So I began to research the nature of the ant. The following is what I found from the National Geographic Web site at that time:

> There are more than 10,000 known ant species around the world. Ants are very determined and organized creatures but in looking at them from the outside, it seems that everything they're doing is chaotic. Ant colonies are headed by queens, and their function is to lay eggs—thousands of eggs. A queen ant can lay as many as 200 eggs within an hour. She lays mostly female ants, which are the worker ants who gather food for the colony

and protect the queen. The male ants are for mating purposes only. The worker ants are wingless and never reproduce. Their job is simply to forage for food, take care of the colony and the queen's eggs, and take care of the nest. In the case of fire ants, their purpose is to build the largest colony possible because the larger the colony, the larger their chances for survival. To accomplish their growth, they often kidnap the ant larvae from other colonies and bring their steal back to the queen. Sometimes, two queens will team up together to build one huge colony. The unfortunate thing, however, is that only one of these queens will survive. Somehow, the other ants in the colony decide which queen they prefer, and then the other queen is killed by decapitation.[5]

Peering at our world situation from the outside, it can seem as if our lives are in complete disarray. The people of the earth are scurrying about, seemingly doing their own thing. We can be tempted to fall into the same pattern when we fail to realize that our steps are being ordered by the Lord. "*The steps of a good man are ordered by the* LORD, *and He delights in his way*" (Psalm 37:23). Try as people may to

There is only one true and living God— the Maker and Healer of individuals, families, nations, and the whole earth.

replace our King with false gods to satisfy their quest for power or other forms of self-gratification, there is and always will remain only one true and living God—the Maker

---

[5] *National Geographic*, http://animals.nationalgeographic.com/animals/bugs/ant. html.

and Healer of individuals, families, nations, and the whole earth.

While my dream depicted the chaos of the world without God as our Leader, ants in the physical world can teach us some important spiritual lessons. The book of Proverbs highlights some of these. The sixth chapter of Proverbs instructs us to consider the ways of the ants to gain wisdom:

> *Go to the ant, you sluggard! Consider her ways and be wise, which, having no captain, overseer or ruler, provides her supplies in the summer, and gathers her food in the harvest.* (Proverbs 6:6–8)

Ants are well prepared for inclement weather. They do not wait for the arrival of bad conditions to gather the things that they need for survival. Likewise, we need to gather spiritual food that will sustain us in these difficult times. The Word of God is our "food"; it is nourishment for our spirits, souls, and bodies.

> *Do not labor for the food which perishes, but for the food which endures to everlasting life, which the Son of Man will give you, because God the Father has set His seal on Him....Most assuredly, I [Jesus] say to you, Moses did not give you the bread from heaven, but My Father gives you the true bread from heaven. For the bread of God is He who comes down from heaven and gives life to the world....I am the bread of life. He who comes to Me shall never hunger, and he who believes in Me shall never thirst.* (John 6:27, 32–33, 35)

> *My food is to do the will of Him who sent Me, and to finish His work.* (John 4:34)

Everyone who partakes only of milk is unskilled in the word of righteousness, for he is a babe. But solid food belongs to those who are of full age, that is, those who by reason of use have their senses exercised to discern both good and evil. (Hebrews 5:13–14)

With my whole heart I have sought You; oh, let me not wander from Your commandments! Your word I have hidden in my heart, that I might not sin against You! Blessed are You, O LORD! Teach me Your statutes! With my lips I have declared all the judgments of Your mouth. I have rejoiced in the way of Your testimonies, as much as in all riches. I will meditate on Your precepts, and contemplate Your ways. I will delight myself in Your statutes; I will not forget Your word. Deal bountifully with Your servant, that I may live and keep Your word. Open my eyes, that I may see wondrous things from Your law....Remember the word to Your servant, upon which You have caused me to hope. This is my comfort in my affliction, for Your word has given me life.
(Psalm 119:10–18, 49–50)

I have not departed from the commandment of His lips; I have treasured the words of His mouth more than my necessary food. (Job 23:12)

We must gather the Word of God into our spirits and build up our *"most holy faith"* (Jude 20). Then, when the devil comes seeking to destroy our spirits, souls, and bodies—the temple of the Holy Spirit—we will already be filled with the Bread of Life.

Furthermore, ants instinctively protect the one who gives them life—the queen—in order to survive. In a similar way, we must always look to God as our Life-giver, Healer, and Sustainer, for He came to give us life more abundantly. (See John 10:10.)

"The ants are a people not strong, yet they prepare" (Proverbs 30:25). Ants are not strong in the sense that they are tiny creatures whose lives could be extinguished in a moment. Yet they have the capacity to carry things that are ten times their body weight. They have endurance and stamina. They put these abilities to good use in preparing for their present and future needs.

We can learn from the ants and realize that spiritual strength and endurance are essential for us in these times.

> *No temptation has overtaken you except such as is common to man; but God is faithful, who will not allow you to be tempted beyond what you are able, but with the temptation will also make the way of escape, that you may be able to bear it.*
>
> (1 Corinthians 10:13)

> *You therefore must endure hardship as a good soldier of Jesus Christ. No one engaged in warfare entangles himself with the affairs of this life, that he may please him who enlisted him as a soldier.*
>
> (2 Timothy 2:3–4)

A Symbol of the Healing of the Nations

When God delivered the Israelites from Egypt, His plan for them included good health. They were a symbol of

God's ultimate plan for the healing of the nations. *"Worship the* LORD *your God, and his blessing will be on your food and water. I will take away sickness from among you, and none will miscarry or be barren in your land. I will give you a full life span"* (Exodus 23:25–26 NIV). While the Israelites wandered about in the wilderness for forty years, their bodies sustained the intensity of the desert sun's rays beating upon their backs. Their clothes and sandals did not wear out, and their feet did not even swell. (See Deuteronomy 8:4; 29:5.) As long as they obeyed God, they remained in good health.

God declared the blessings for obedience to His Word. These blessings are relevant to our lives today.

In Deuteronomy 28:1–13, God declared the blessings the Israelites would receive for obedience to His Word as they lived in the Promised Land. These blessings are relevant to our lives today as God's children. When you arise each morning, personalize them by speaking them over yourself. Put them into the context of your life. For example, the "basket" and "kneading bowl" refer to God's provision of food.

+ "Blessed shall I be in the city, and blessed shall I be in the country." (See verse 3.)

+ "Blessed shall be the fruit of my body, the produce of my ground, and the increase of my herds." (See verse 4.)

+ "Blessed shall be my basket and my kneading bowl." (See verse 5.)

+ "Blessed shall I be when I come in, and blessed shall I be when I go out." (See verse 6.)

+ "The Lord will cause my enemies who rise against me to be defeated before my face; they shall come out against me one way and flee before me seven ways." (See verse 7.)

+ "The Lord will command the blessing on me in my storehouses and in all to which I set my hand, and He will bless me in the land which the Lord my God is giving me." (See verse 8.)

+ "The Lord will establish me as a holy [man/woman] to Himself, just as He has sworn to me, if I keep the commandments of the Lord my God and walk in His ways. Then all peoples of the earth shall see that I am called by the name of the Lord, and they shall be afraid of me." (See verses 9–10.)

+ "And the Lord will grant me plenty of goods, in the fruit of my body, in the increase of my livestock, and in the produce of my ground, in the land of which the Lord swore to my fathers to give me." (See verse 11.)

+ "The Lord will open to me His good treasure, the heavens, to give the rain to my land in its season, and to bless all the work of my hand." (See verse 12.)

+ "I shall lend to many nations, but I shall not borrow." (See verse 12.)

+ "And the Lord will make me the head and not the tail; I shall be above only, and not be beneath, if I heed the commandments of the Lord my God and am careful to observe them." (See verse 13.)

Just as God wanted to bless the Israelites in every way possible, He wants to bless you today. He wants to bless you with health, give you peace of mind, and prosper you abundantly.

God's Compassion and Healing

God's plans for the healing for the nations are a result of His compassion:

> For God so loved the world that He gave His only begotten Son, that whoever believes in Him should not perish but have everlasting life. For God did not send His Son into the world to condemn the world, but that the world through Him might be saved.
> (John 3:16–17)

Jesus didn't just talk about healing; He went about doing the Father's business in fulfillment of His purpose.

> So Jesus stood still and called them [the two blind men], and said, "What do you want Me to do for you?" They said to Him, "Lord, that our eyes may be opened." So Jesus had compassion and touched their eyes. And immediately their eyes received sight, and they followed Him.   (Matthew 20:32–34)

> When evening had come, they brought to Him many who were demon-possessed. And He cast out the spirits with a word, and healed all who were sick, that it might be fulfilled which was spoken by Isaiah the prophet, saying: "He Himself took our infirmities and bore our sicknesses."   (Matthew 8:16–17)

No longer do we have to bear the burden of something that Jesus has already taken from us. That is why it is vitally important to repeat the Word of God until it becomes a reality for you rather than simply words. Many in the body of Christ have become dull to the Scriptures—the very Word that holds the power to overcome sicknesses and diseases.

God is often unfairly portrayed as a dictator or someone who is sitting around waiting for people to sin so that He can strike them down. This depiction is contrary to His Word and nature. *"But You, O Lord, are a God full of compassion, and gracious, longsuffering and abundant in mercy and truth"* (Psalm 86:15). *"Praise be to the God and Father of our Lord Jesus Christ, the Father of compassion and the God of all comfort, who comforts us in all our troubles"* (2 Corinthians 1:3–4 NIV).

Jesus was and still is a God of compassion. Throughout the Gospels, we see that people brought the plight of their sick loved ones to Jesus, and He healed them. (See, for example, Mark 5:22–24; 35–43.) He is the same God today that He was in biblical times. *"Jesus Christ is the same yesterday, today, and forever"* (Hebrews 13:8). Bring your sicknesses to Jesus and allow the Word that He speaks over your situation to manifest your healing in the natural. Be healed, be set free, be delivered, in Jesus' name.

Be healed, be set free, be delivered, in Jesus' name.

Finally, remember the word that God spoke to King Solomon:

> *When I shut up heaven and there is no rain, or command the locusts to devour the land, or send pestilence among My people, if My people who are called by My name will humble themselves, and pray and seek My*

face, and turn from their wicked ways, then I will hear from heaven, and will forgive their sin and heal their land.   (2 Chronicles 7:13–14)

Trusting in God's love and compassion, maintaining a humble attitude, praying with sincerity, seeking God and His will, and practicing true repentance lead to forgiveness and healing.

1-800-636-0910

Health Market. com

EPILOGUE

"You did not choose Me, but I chose you and appointed you
that you should go and bear fruit,
and that your fruit should remain, that whatever you ask the
Father in My name He may give you."
—John 15:16

Life has a way of sneaking up on us and delivering unexpected news that we are ill-equipped to handle—or so it seems. Sometimes, the news can be so devastating that we pray, "Lord, did You know about this, and if so, why did You allow this to happen to me?" We find ourselves questioning God, as Job did when it seemed as if he would perish along with his children. The truth is that we do not always receive clear-cut answers from God about the "whys." Yet one thing remains certain: God is continually occupied with meeting our needs. *"The LORD longs to be gracious to you; he rises to show you compassion. For the LORD is a God of justice. Blessed are all who wait for him!"* (Isaiah 30:18 NIV).

God Is Able to Deliver

God is earnestly concerned with your well-being. Don't give up on Him, and don't give up on your healing. It may not always seem like it, but God is always with us, working out His plans for our lives. Sometimes, it is the trials we go through that push us into our God-given purposes.

God is always with us, working out His plans for our lives.

This process can seem so inconvenient compared to the normal processes of life that there are times when, if we did not persevere in God, we might gladly trade in our destinies for a moment of relief. If God allowed us to sneak a peek at the process through which He will take us to reach His purposes, then we well might answer Him with, "Thanks, but no thanks." That is why life is revealed to us in increments. Rarely does God show us the entire picture all at once. He reveals His will in phases, and, by faith, we step out and receive His blessings. Sometimes, these blessings seem to come easily, but other times, we will not receive them without a fight. *"The kingdom of heaven suffers violence, and the violent take it by force"* (Matthew 11:12).

There are times when we have all felt as if God has forgotten us, especially in the thick of the battle. Yet God's ways are not our ways, and He has already answered every question that we could have before the foundation of the earth. Likewise, He has also already provided for our healings. The enemy desires to derail us, however, by convincing us that God has forgotten all about us and that He no longer cares about our situations. Though it can seem like a difficult task to continue believing God in the midst of your crisis, it is a must. Giving up is never an option.

When King Nebuchadnezzar of Babylon threatened Shadrach, Meshach, and Abed-Nego because they refused to bow down to his image, it seemed as if life for them was over. Nonetheless, even as they were walking to their deaths, they refused to bow. Instead, they answered,

> *Our God whom we serve is able to deliver us from the burning fiery furnace, and He will deliver us from your hand, O king. But if not, let it be known to you, O king, that we do not serve your gods, nor will we worship the gold image which you have set up.*
>
> (Daniel 3:17–18)

We must echo this response when the devil comes to entice us. We must not bow to the devil's devices. Instead, we must continue to believe God and tell the devil, "The God whom I serve is able to deliver me!"

It wasn't until Shadrach, Meshach, and Abed-Nego were thrown into the fiery furnace that they were delivered. (See verses 23–27.) Talk about last-minute miracles! Nothing is impossible with God. When the devil approaches you and whispers that God does not care or that He has forgotten about your need, fight him with the Word of God. It is not that God has forgotten about you but that the devil has intensified his fight against you.

The negative has a tendency to overwhelm us at exactly the moment when we need God the most. The devil knows that if we yield to God and continue fighting against his devices, we will come out victorious. It often seems, therefore, that right when God is about to bless us with the miracle that we need, the devil heightens his attacks. The sad part is that many people give up right at the brink of receiving the miracle they so desperately need. Our prayer is that you will heed the advice of James 4:7–8: *"Submit to God. Resist the devil and he will flee from you. Draw near to God and He will draw near to you."* Sometimes, God allows us to get right in the midst of the fire before He delivers us, but that doesn't mean it is too late!

The Reality, Power, and Necessity of Healing

God wants to lift us up higher in Him and in His purposes for us.

God wants to lift us up higher in Him and in His purposes for us. If we want to bring back healing into the church and as a witness to the world, we have to begin as individuals to believe that God has the power to heal. If we want to win the lost and heal the sick, we must pray diligently and with perseverance. As you believe and walk in the Word of the Lord, then the power of God's Spirit, as depicted in Isaiah 61, will start to be manifest in your life:

> *The Spirit of the Lord God is upon Me, because the Lord has anointed Me to preach good tidings to the poor; He has sent Me to heal the brokenhearted, to proclaim liberty to the captives, and the opening of the prison to those who are bound; to proclaim the acceptable year of the Lord, and the day of vengeance of our God; to comfort all who mourn, to console those who mourn in Zion, to give them beauty for ashes, the oil of joy for mourning, the garment of praise for the spirit*

of heaviness; that they may be called trees of righteous-
ness, the planting of the LORD, *that He may be glori-*
fied. (Isaiah 61:1–3)

Look at what God gives to us and to those to whom we
minister through His loving Spirit:

+ Beauty for ashes.

+ The oil of joy for mourning.

+ The garment of praise for the spirit of heaviness.

"If anyone is in Christ, he is a new creation; old things
have passed away; behold, all things have become new. Now
all things are of God, who has reconciled us to Himself through
Jesus Christ" (2 Corinthians 5:17–18). Whatever you are
going through is covered by the blood of the Lamb. God
left nothing out, because He is concerned about whatever
concerns you. Hallelujah!

Give God the hindrances of your mind and the things
that make you sad in life, so that He may replace your tormenting thoughts with peace and tranquility. Give Him
your pain and sicknesses, so that He may bring healing.
Receive His power to minister that same peace and healing
to others from the ailments of life that the devil sends to
destroy them. Remember that everything you go through
in life is an opportunity to glorify God: *"that [you] may be*
called trees of righteousness, the planting of the LORD, *that He*
may be glorified" (Isaiah 61:3).

The Word of the Lord in Isaiah gives us another anal-
ogy, as well. It compares how a bride and bridegroom take
great care in their appearance to how the Lord clothes
those who have committed themselves to Him:

> *I will greatly rejoice in the* Lord, *my soul shall be joyful in my God; for He has clothed me with the garments of salvation, He has covered me with the robe of righteousness, as a bridegroom decks himself with ornaments, and as a bride adorns herself with her jewels.* (Isaiah 61:10)

+ He clothes you with the garments of salvation.
+ He covers you with the robe of righteousness.

Once you are "decked out" for God, the world can see His glory revealed in you. Many will come to you desiring prayer and healing, and you will be prepared because you will allow the Scriptures and the Spirit of the Lord to guide you.

The early believers had a type of faith that enabled them to believe in healings and other miraculous works—even that the dead could be raised.

> *Assuredly, I say to you, whoever says to this mountain, "Be removed and be cast into the sea," and does not doubt in his heart, but believes that those things he says will be done, he will have whatever he says. Therefore I say to you, whatever things you ask when you pray, believe that you receive them, and you will have them.* (Mark 11:23–24)

Who but God could restore damaged brain cells, make sicknesses dry up instantly, cause addictions to cease, and so forth? There is no ailment you can imagine for which God does not have a cure.

Again, a great influx of people will come to the church seeking to know more about the Healer whom we confess.

We must prepare ourselves now to receive those whom God is about to send us for healing. We can no longer supply people with watered-down answers, which cause them to leave in disappointment. Immerse yourself in the Word of God, strengthen your faith, *"pray with the spirit, and... pray with the understanding"* (1 Corinthians 14:15), and He will send those across your path to whom you can minister healing. When you do not know how to pray, the Spirit will pray for you:

> *Likewise the Spirit also helps in our weaknesses. For we do not know what we should pray for as we ought, but the Spirit Himself makes intercession for us with groanings which cannot be uttered.* (Romans 8:26)

The early church understood the reality, the power, and the necessity of supernatural healing. It is now incumbent upon the twenty-first-century church to carry forward this torch and to leave it as an inheritance for our children's children.

YOUR DECLARATION OF FAITH FOR HEALING

God has already sent His Word to heal me. I confess today that He is my Healer and that He is healing my ailment right now. I am living by His Spirit, and I allow His Spirit to take over my entire being. Jesus is the Lord, my Physician. His Word is life to me and health to my flesh. In the name of Jesus, I cast off every ailment that is debilitating me spiritually, mentally, emotionally, and physically. This is a new day—a day of health, peace of mind, and wealth. Nothing can separate me from the love of God or from His divine will and purpose for my life. I receive the miracle that God has preordained for me. Lord, I thank You for turning sickness away from me and for allowing no disease to rest in my body. I thank You for complete and total healing. In Jesus' name, amen.

(For Scriptures referred to in this declaration, see Psalm 107:19, Proverbs 4:22, and Romans 8:35–39.)

Healing Scriptures

I am the LORD who heals you.   (Exodus 15:26)

Blessed is the man who walks not in the counsel of the ungodly, nor stands in the path of sinners, nor sits in the seat of the scornful; but his delight is in the law of the LORD, and in His law he meditates day and night. He shall be like a tree planted by the rivers of water, that brings forth its fruit in its season, whose leaf also shall not wither; and whatever he does shall prosper.
(Psalm 1:1–3)

Then they cried out to the LORD in their trouble, and He saved them out of their distresses. He sent His word and healed them, and delivered them from their destructions. Oh, that men would give thanks to the LORD for His goodness, and for His wonderful works to the children of men!   (Psalm 107:19–21)

O LORD my God, I cried out to You, and You healed me. LORD, You brought my soul up from the grave;

You have kept me alive, that I should not go down to the pit. (Psalm 30:2–3)

My son, give attention to my words; incline your ear to my sayings. Do not let them depart from your eyes; keep them in the midst of your heart; for they are life to those who find them, and health to all their flesh. (Proverbs 4:20–22)

Is this not the fast that I have chosen: to loose the bonds of wickedness, to undo the heavy burdens, to let the oppressed go free, and that you break every yoke? Is it not to share your bread with the hungry, and that you bring to your house the poor who are cast out; when you see the naked, that you cover him, and not hide yourself from your own flesh? Then your light shall break forth like the morning, your healing shall spring forth speedily, and your righteousness shall go before you; the glory of the LORD shall be your rear guard. Then you shall call, and the LORD will answer; you shall cry, and He will say, "Here I am." (Isaiah 58:6–9)

"For I will restore health to you and heal you of your wounds," says the LORD. (Jeremiah 30:17)

Behold, I will bring it health and healing; I will heal them and reveal to them the abundance of peace and truth. (Jeremiah 33:6)

As you go, preach, saying, "The kingdom of heaven is at hand." Heal the sick, cleanse the lepers, raise the dead, cast out demons. Freely you have received, freely give. (Matthew 10:7–8)

The Spirit of the LORD is upon Me, because He has anointed Me to preach the gospel to the poor; He has sent Me to heal the brokenhearted, to proclaim liberty to the captives and recovery of sight to the blind, to set at liberty those who are oppressed.   (Luke 4:18)

And the whole multitude sought to touch Him, for power went out from Him and healed them all.
(Luke 6:19)

Most assuredly, I say to you, he who believes in Me, the works that I do he will do also; and greater works than these he will do, because I go to My Father. And whatever you ask in My name, that I will do, that the Father may be glorified in the Son. If you ask anything in My name, I will do it.   (John 14:12–14)

Confess your trespasses to one another, and pray for one another, that you may be healed. The effective, fervent prayer of a righteous man avails much.
(James 5:16)

Who Himself bore our sins in His own body on the tree, that we, having died to sins, might live for righteousness; by whose stripes you were healed.
(1 Peter 2:24)

Beloved, I pray that you may prosper in all things and be in health, just as your soul prospers.   (3 John 1:2)

About the Authors

Mary K. Baxter

Mary K. Baxter was born in Chattanooga, Tennessee. When she was a girl, her mother taught her about Jesus Christ and His salvation. Although she felt called by God at that time, she was truly born again when she was a young woman and God revealed Himself to her as Savior at the same time He miraculously healed her newborn child.

In 1976, while Mary was living in Belleville, Michigan, Jesus appeared to her in human form, in dreams, visions, and revelations. During those visits, He revealed to her the depths, degrees, levels, and torments of lost souls in hell, telling her that this message is for the whole world. Since that time, she has received many visitations from the Lord. In God's wisdom, to give balance to her message, she has also received many visions, dreams, and revelations of heaven, angels, and the end of time.

On Mary's tours of hell, she walked with Jesus and talked with many people. Jesus showed her what happens to unrepentant souls when they die and what happens to servants of God when they do not remain obedient to their calling, go back into a life of sin, and refuse to repent.

Mary was ordained as a minister in 1983 at a Full Gospel church in Taylor, Michigan, and recently received a Doctor of Ministry degree from Faith Bible College, Independence, Missouri. Ministers, leaders, and saints of the Lord around the world speak very highly of her and her ministry. The movement of the Holy Spirit is emphasized in all her services, and many miracles have occurred in them. The gifts of the Holy Spirit with demonstrations of power and healing are manifested in her meetings as the Spirit of God leads and empowers her.

Mary, a mother and grandmother, loves the Lord with everything she has—all her heart, mind, soul, and strength. She is truly a dedicated handmaiden of the Lord, and she desires above all to be a soulwinner for Jesus Christ. From the headquarters of Divine Revelation, Inc., her Florida-based ministry, this anointed evangelist continues to travel the world, speaking at conferences, seminars, and other gatherings and telling her story of heaven and hell and her revelatory visits from the Lord.

For speaking engagements, please contact:
Dr. Mary K. Baxter
Divine Revelation, Inc.
P.O. Box 121524
West Melbourne, FL 32912-1524
e-mail: marykbaxter@yahoo.com
www.marykbaxterinc.com

www.Isaiah 58. TV

George G. Bloomer

Bishop George Bloomer is the founder and senior pastor of Bethel Family Worship Center, a multicultural congregation in Durham, North Carolina, and The Life Church in Goldsboro, North Carolina. A native of Brooklyn, New York, Bloomer overcame difficult personal challenges, as well as a destructive environment of poverty and drugs, and he uses those learning experiences as priceless tools for empowering others to excel beyond their seeming limitations.

He has appeared as a guest on several television, radio, and media outlets nationwide, including CNN's *Faces of Faith*, the Trinity Broadcasting Network, *The Harvest Show* (LeSEA Broadcasting), and *The 700 Club* (Christian Broadcasting Network). He can be seen weekly on his nationally broadcast program *Spiritual Authority*.

Bloomer is the author of a number of books, including *More of Him*, *Authority Abusers*, and the national best seller, *Witchcraft in the Pews*. He has also collaborated with Mary K. Baxter on *A Divine Revelation of Deliverance* and *A Divine Revelation of Prayer*.

He conducts many seminars dealing with relationships, finances, stress management, and spiritual warfare. In addition, he travels extensively as a conference speaker, delivering a message to liberate and impact the lives of thousands for Christ.

Bishop Bloomer was awarded an honorary Doctor of Divinity degree from Christian Outreach Bible Institute.

1-800-981-1613
stJude